UNSAFE STREETS

Street homelessness and crime

Scott Ballintyne

IPPR

30-32 Southampton St
London WC2E 7RA
Tel: 020 7470 6100
Fax: 020 7470 6111
info@ippr.org.uk
www.ippr.org.uk
Registered charity 800065

The Institute for Public Policy Research is an independent charity whose purpose is to contribute to public understanding of social, economic and political questions through research, discussion and publication. It was established in 1988 by leading figures in the academic, business and trade-union communities to provide an alternative to the free market think tanks.

IPPR's research agenda reflects the challenges facing Britain and Europe. Current programmes cover the areas of economic and industrial policy, Europe, governmental reform, human rights, defence, social policy, the environment and media issues.

Besides its programme of research and publication, IPPR also provides a forum for political and trade union leaders, academic experts and those from business, finance, government and the media, to meet and discuss issues of common concern.

Trustees

Production & design by **EMPHASIS**
ISBN 1 86030 091 X

Printed and bound in Great Britain by
Biddles Ltd, Guildford and King's Lynn

Contents

Acknowledgments

Many people and not a few organisations have given generously of their time, efforts and expertise to this investigation. Crisis, the national homelessness charity, initiated the idea and provided the funding to make it happen. Kate Tomlinson and Shaks Ghosh stuck with it when it grew larger than first expected and showed patience in awaiting the findings. Without the many people who supported the investigation and took part, the extent of victimisation would remain hidden and an opportunity to reduce it would be missed. Rough-sleepers, street outreach workers, community organisations and police officers in Glasgow, Swansea and London showed time and again their willingness to try to work together to tackle deep-rooted and complex problems. No-one, least of all those who sleep rough, underestimates the harshness of street homelessness or the part which crime plays in making it harder to leave the streets.

This independent investigation was funded by CRISIS, the leading national homelessness charity, as part of its research programme on homelessness. The views expressed are those of the author and not necessarily those of IPPR, Crisis, their staff or trustees.

For Maggie, for 20 years of having a roof over our heads and for always keeping me included.

About the author

Scott Ballintyne is a Research Associate at the Institute for Public Policy Research. Previously he was a senior manager in local government and has twenty years experience in policing and community safety. He now lives in Los Angeles and can be contacted at scottballintyne@compuserve.com.

CRISIS
WORKING FOR HOMELESS PEOPLE
Charity number 1036533

Preface

Shaks Ghosh, Chief Executive, Crisis

"I was sleeping in my sleeping bag. I woke up, someone hit me with a baseball bat. My friend Paul he got kicked to death and he was only 24."

Every night hundreds of people sleep rough, exposed not only to the damaging experience on their health and general wellbeing of living on the street, but also to the very real threat of attack. Nearly four in five have been victims of crime; compare this to the one in five young men who are attacked – the group most at risk of attack in the general population – and it highlights how vulnerable rough sleepers are.

This victimisation is a problem that needs to be tackled. Today, people sleeping rough have a complex array of needs: from mental health to drugs and alcohol. Understandably, police aren't keen to lock them up and throw away the key. But without the resources they need, what option do they have?

Out of all of the agencies, statutory and voluntary, the police are likely to have the most contact with rough sleepers when they patrol the streets. But they are currently in a no-win situation and their approach is 'move them on or take them in', while alternative policing methods such as the zero tolerance approach as practiced in New York and Miami have to-date been met with suspicion and alarm.

Unsafe Streets clearly demonstrates the important role of and positive opportunities the police to provide real support to rough sleepers. Instead of being 'churned' through the system and ending up back on the streets, the police could direct them to detox or to diversionary schemes. The Charing Cross Homeless Unit is just one example of how a supportive approach has been adopted to great success.

Unsafe Streets draws parallels between the hidden levels of victimisation being experienced by rough-sleepers and how we used to respond inadequately to racial harassment and violence against women. The recommendations it makes follow similar solutions – to tackle the problems we need to realise partnerships agencies, namely between the police and street homelessness agencies. But they have to be supported.

List of figures & tables

Summary

Background to the investigation

This summary sets out the main findings and recommendations from an investigation into street homelessness and crime which explored rough-sleepers as victims of crime, offending by rough-sleepers and contact between rough-sleepers and the police. Little was known about the experiences of rough-sleepers as victims of crime or the nature and extent of their contact with police. There was slightly more information about rough-sleepers as offenders, particularly when begging, but such information has tended to exist in isolation from policy-making and, with few exceptions, has not had a consistent impact upon day to day service delivery.

This, in part, reflects the social exclusion of people who sleep rough. Rough-sleepers are not covered by the British Crime Survey, which provides a broader understanding of victimisation in the UK and increasingly informs public policy-making on victimisation and crime reduction. It is understandable, yet it leaves a gap in our knowledge of rough-sleeping and may miss an important context which influences rough-sleepers' involvement in offending and their contact with police. More importantly, it may miss an opportunity to intervene constructively and help rough-sleepers leave the street.

The investigation set out to answer a number of questions.

- Of what crimes are rough-sleepers victims? How often are they victims? Do they report victimisation to the police? How does their experience compare to that of the wider community?
- What offences are committed by people who sleep rough? Why do they offend? How often does this offending lead to police contact? What are the most common outcomes for rough-sleepers when they offend?
- How much contact is there between rough-sleepers and the police? How does this contact come about? How do UK police forces police street homelessness? Have UK police forces developed any particular policies or practices for policing rough-sleepers?

The aim was to provide reliable information on victimisation, offending and the policing of street homelessness to complement and inform the wider drive to tackle social exclusion and to identify practical ways of intervening constructively to support rough-sleepers, address their needs and help them move off the streets.

The fieldwork took place between May and December 1998 in Glasgow, Swansea and London. The investigation included: group discussions and 120 in-depth interviews with rough-sleepers; a series of round table discussions with front-line service deliverers and voluntary organisations; interviews with police officers, including beat and community constables, local operational commanders and senior police management; a review of policy and practice across all UK police forces.

The following sections summarise the findings and their implications. There are a number of important recommendations for better planning and co-ordination between services and agencies – now a recurring feature of the drive to tackle social exclusion. The main report explores the issues in detail.

We need to reduce the hidden level of victimisation being experienced by rough-sleepers and intervene constructively when they have offended to divert them, where appropriate, out of the criminal justice system and into alternatives which can help them leave the streets. There are parallels between the hidden levels of victimisation being experienced by rough sleepers now and how agencies and services used to respond inadequately to racial harassment and violence against women.

As a starting point we need to ensure that alternatives to the street are safer than the street. Despite the high levels of victimisation experienced by rough-sleepers, it does not necessarily follow that anywhere available to them is safer than sleeping on the streets. Rough-sleepers repeatedly express their concern that many hostels and much temporary accommodation is less safe than the streets. At the same time we could learn some useful lessons from recent multi-agency work on domestic violence and racial harassment which have developed constructive ways of building confidence amongst victims, increasing reporting and providing support services to meet victims' needs. These apply at point of contact and as ongoing support.

Police and particularly the courts need to be integrated more consistently and effectively into local planning and service delivery. This would potentially widen local policing options beyond enforcement and widen court options beyond the revolving door of low level offending which is of little benefit to rough-sleepers, the criminal justice system or the wider community. Although there is some evidence that the Rough Sleepers' Initiative (RSI) has improved connections between police and other agencies, with few exceptions, the police role remains peripheral and mainly reactive. The court role remains largely unconnected. There seems to be an opportunity to intervene constructively in the offending cycle which is currently being missed. Homelessness agencies could play a part in developing, piloting and delivering appropriate interventions and support.

Rough-sleepers as victims of crime

Street homeless people in the UK experience hidden levels of unreported victimisation, particularly:

- *a high level of criminal victimisation:* 78 per cent have been victims of crime on at least one occasion during their last period of sleeping rough
- *a high level of crimes against the person:* 52 per cent have been victims of personal theft, 45 per cent of common assault and 35 per cent have been wounded on at least one occasion
- *repeated victimisation:* 62 per cent have been repeatedly verbally harassed; 53 per cent repeatedly threatened; 42 per cent repeatedly stolen from, and 39 per cent assaulted more than once
- *a low level of reporting to police:* 21 per cent of incidents were reported to police
- *a high level of fear of crime:* 69 per cent of rough-sleepers report that they are afraid of being a victim of crime

In comparison, the British Crime Survey (1998) found that 1 in 3 adults (34 per cent) in England and Wales had been victims of crime at least once and that the majority of those crimes were against property. Within the general population the highest at risk group from crimes against the person is young men, 1 in 5 of whom (21 per cent) has been a victim of a crime against the person. It also found that 44 per cent of incidents were reported to police.

Rough-sleepers are victims of crimes against the person, often repeatedly, which are reported infrequently to the police. The level of personal victimisation far exceeds that of the wider population, even the most at risk groups, such as young men.

Victimisation comes from the general public and from within the street homeless community. The majority of verbal harassment (64 per cent), threatening behaviour (56 per cent) and wounding (63 per cent) comes from the general public. Assault, theft from the person, robbery and extortion are almost equally as likely to come from the public and other street homeless people.

Rough-sleepers as offenders

Street homeless people in the UK report high levels of minor offending whilst sleeping rough, particularly:

- *a high level of overall offending*: 85 per cent of rough-sleepers report that they have committed at least one offence during their last period of sleeping rough
- *a high level of minor offending, the most common being theft from shops and public order offences*: 72 per cent report theft from shops and 62 per cent report minor public order offences
- *a high level of repeat offending:* 80 per cent of those who have offended report that they have offended on more than one occasion
- *a high level of police involvement once an offence has been committed:* 82 per cent of those committing a minor order offence and 73 per cent of those stealing from shops have come into police contact because of the offending
- *a high level of formal processing once an offence been committed:* 80 per cent of those stealing from shops and 60 per cent of those involved in minor public order offending report that they were charged and sentenced

Police figures and interviews support a pattern of rough-sleepers as frequent, repeat, low level offenders who have a high level of contact with officers in particular areas. Although rough-sleepers do commit more serious offences, this is less common. The overall level of formal processing is high and repeated.

Two main reasons are given by rough-sleepers for their offending. For public order offences the main reason is force of circumstance, becoming caught up in an incident in public; and for theft from shops the stated reason is need.

The high level of police involvement appears to stem from a combination of the frequency of offending and rough-sleepers' lifestyle in the public eye. The findings support earlier studies which showed that street homeless people are not regular perpetrators of serious offences, are not serious predatory criminals and are more likely to be engaged in lower level nuisance offending rather than being a serious threat to life or property. Some habitual criminals do appear amongst street homeless peoplc, mainly through downward drift, but street homelessness itself is as substantial a source of police contact as deliberate criminal behaviour.

The overall picture is one of high levels of repeat minor offending which leads to formal processing once police are involved and results in a revolving door in and out of the criminal justice system. The most frequent offences are by-products of rough-sleeping – minor public order and theft from shops. This being the case, offending by people who sleep rough and their subsequent involvement in the criminal justice system, appears to be an opportunity to intervene positively to reduce offending, divert minor offenders and support rough-sleepers coming off the street. We are currently missing this opportunity.

Policing people who sleep rough

Street homeless people in the UK have high levels of contact with police. Few police forces have developed particular strategies or policies for policing rough-sleepers, primarily because it is not seen as a significant policing issue within the force area. The investigation explored two aspects of policing street homelessness – contact between rough-sleepers and police and policing policies and practices across the UK.

The main findings on contact between rough-sleepers and police show:

- *a high level of overall contact between rough-sleepers and police:* 87 per cent of rough-sleepers report contact with the police on at least one occasion during the most recent period when they have been street homeless
- *a high level of police initiated contact:* 70 per cent of rough sleepers had contact arising whilst police were on patrol, 58 per cent whilst involved in an incident, 48 per cent whilst drinking in public, and 49 per cent whilst asleep at night
- *a lower level of rough-sleeper initiated contact:* 26 per cent of rough-sleepers had initiated contact with police because they needed assistance
- *a high level of dissatisfaction amongst rough-sleepers about police contact*: 42 per cent of rough-sleepers were very dissatisfied with their contact with police, possibly reflecting the high levels for formal contact leading to arrest and charge

The findings on policing policies and practices on street homelessness show:

- *street homelessness is not a local policing issue for many forces* because the overall number of rough-sleepers is low (34 of the 45 forces which responded to the review reported that street homelessness was not a significant policing issue within the force area)
- *against this backdrop:*
  - no forces specifically record offences against or by rough-sleepers
  - few have adopted a specific policy or strategy for policing street homelessness (where there are policies they are derived from two sources: RSI-related work or force service equality statements)
  - little specific training is given to officers (what training there is stems from two sources: general probationer training or personal skills training)
  - there are few policing initiatives directed at street homeless people; the expectation is that officers will deal with issues as part of the daily policing of an area

- *where there is seen to be a policing issue, mainly because there are higher numbers of street homeless people or there is a perceived public nuisance, three policing styles appear to dominate:*
    - enforcement policing (where rough-sleeping is policed as part of wider, high profile public policing and officers influence the public presence of street homeless people through tackling begging, drinking in public places, moving people on and on occasion seeking bail conditions to exclude rough-sleepers from particular public areas)
    - supportive, graded policing (where officers provide advice on support services and apply informal cautions, formal cautions and arrest as a means of regulating the public activities and behaviour of rough-sleepers both in relation to the public and within the homeless community)
    - individualised policing (where community or beat officers are expected to take local responsibility for managing, containing or reducing any policing issues within their area arising from rough-sleeping)
- *police involvement in RSI and multi-agency work on rough-sleeping appears to be increasing slowly* (but few forces have formal involvement as partners in RSI and multi-agency projects are more likely to be one-off, time limited responses rather than problem-solving programmes)

The overall picture is of frequent contact between rough-sleepers and police, often formal, most often police initiated and leading to dissatisfaction amongst street homeless people. At the same time, with a few exceptions, the policing of street homeless people is not a significant policing issue nor one which engages police in significant multi-agency work. Outside those few areas which are developing some multi-agency policing responses to street homelessness, the main policing response appears to be a mix of enforcement in response to public quality of life and delegation to individual officers to respond locally.

The aim must be twofold: to promote consistency and good practice across police forces and to widen policing options beyond enforcement into partnership. This is not to say that enforcement is not an essential ingredient in policing street homelessness but that an over-reliance upon enforcement often goes hand in hand with a lack of multi-agency partnership options. Evidence suggests that we are slow in developing policing partnership options and that this is not helping us to meet the target of reducing the overall numbers of rough-sleepers in the UK.

The 2002 target for reducing street homelessness requires new approaches in policing and a speedy uplift to police involvement in local multi-agency programmes both strategically and operationally. There appears to be little appetite across police forces for 'zero tolerance' policing of street homelessness. Most officers do not see policing as the primary answer to street homelessness. There are a number of policing initiatives, for example, the street homelessness unit within the Metropolitan Police and the city centre joint work between Swansea Police and the *Big Issue* (Cymru), which offer emerging good practice.

Making improvements: rough-sleeper and police views on priorities

These are the views of those who live and work on the street. They are not always comfortable or easily accommodated. They are essentially practical views which address the immediacy of their situation but they are important benchmarks for rough-sleepers and police. They have to be incorporated into service design and any wider proposals on victim support, intervention, diversion, crime reduction and partnership if those proposals are to have any currency amongst police officers and rough-sleepers. Listening to their wishes is a litmus test for the seriousness with which we are tackling social exclusion.

Street homeless people offered the view that the levels of victimisation and offending could be reduced by:

- providing safe places, with or without a roof, where they could sleep at night
- providing accessible, secure places to leave belongings
- regular access to food and support services, such as laundry and housing advice

Contact with the police could be improved by:

- providing training for police officers on street homelessness

- setting up more self-help initiatives similar to the *Big Issue*
- establishing a special police homelessness team or contact point whom they could trust

Police officers seek three changes to help reduce victimisation and offending and to assist them in the policing of street homelessness, namely:

- other agencies providing services for street homeless people across the 24-hour day to give officers wider options than arrest
- drug and alcohol detoxification facilities to enable police to divert rough-sleepers with drink and drug related problems away from police cells and into more appropriate support services
- a means of contacting other services quickly and reliably so that there is a possibility of intervention rather than circulating rough-sleepers through the system

These views have merit not just because they are rooted in daily experience but because they offer practical keys to help rough-sleepers help themselves and to widen the options available to police officers so they can provide a better service.

Implications and recommendations

Three major features dominate rough-sleepers' experiences of crime: high, unrecorded levels of repeated personal victimisation; frequent, minor public order offending stemming from life in the public eye and repeated theft from shops, justified by rough-sleepers as stemming from need; and, regular contact with police leading to a revolving door relationship with the criminal justice system.

Similar features dominate police officers' landscapes: regular contact with rough-sleepers arising from repeated, low level offending accompanied by a lack of options for dealing with offenders, particularly those with drug and alcohol related problems, and a consequent continuous processing through the criminal justice system without a longer term solution.

The investigation has helped to identify the scale of the issues for both rough-sleepers and police. It reinforces the need for co-ordinated, multi-agency work and suggests the direction being pursued on social exclusion is essentially valid. Detailed implications and recommend-ations are set out in the main report, but three issues stand above all others:

- that we are dealing with levels of unreported personal victimisation amongst rough-sleepers akin to previous 'hidden problems' with racial harassment and violence against women and which need to be addressed as part of any package to help people come off the streets
- that we are missing an opportunity to divert rough-sleepers away from offending and off the streets when we fail to intervene and provide useful alternatives to their revolving door relationship with the criminal justice system
- that we need to improve police involvement in strategic multi-agency work on street homelessness to provide more consistent, wider policing options than enforcement for policing street homelessness

The findings have implications for how we design services; for how we deliver services; and, for how agencies work together to reduce victimisation and encourage a transition from the streets.

The recommendations are:

Tackling victimisation

Improving rough-sleepers' safety

Recommendation 1

The Department for the Environment, Transport and the Regions (DETR) and the Home Office should set up a multi-agency short-life task group to review safety in hostels and temporary accommodation and bring forward recommended standards and good practice for improving personal safety for rough-sleepers in such accommodation.

Recommendation 2

Local street homelessness co-ordinating groups or in their absence local community safety partnerships should set up a joint review of safety in local hostels and temporary accommodation involving police, local authority housing and social services, and street homelessness agencies.

Recommendation 3

DETR and the Home Office in partnership with police forces and local street homelessness co-ordinating groups should establish a pilot Safe Havens programme in a small number of urban areas to develop best practice multi-agency packages for protecting rough-sleepers and reducing victimisation.

Recommendation 4

All police forces should include an assessment of police patrolling patterns in areas where rough-sleepers congregate and bring forward proposals to increase informal contact between officers and people who are street homeless within a wider review of the policing of street homelessness across the force area.

Reducing personal victimisation and supporting rough-sleepers as victims

Recommendation 5

Local street homelessness co-ordinating groups or in their absence local community safety partnership groups should come together with local victim support to:

- establish local inter-agency victim support services for street homeless people;
- prioritise a reduction in crimes of violence against rough-sleepers;
- set up repeat victimisation packages to tackle prevalent victimisation of rough-sleepers in the local area.

Recommendation 6

Street homeless service providers should review the needs of people who sleep rough in their area and consider how best to provide secure places for rough-sleepers to leave personal belongings alongside existing service provision.

Increasing rough-sleepers' reporting of victimisation

Recommendation 7

Street homelessness co-ordinating groups should include, as part of the local strategy for reducing rough-sleeping, a victimisation reporting programme which requires local front-line agencies to record victim incidents involving rough-sleepers and provides a published network of contact points for accessing victim support services.

Improving connections between street homelessness and community safety services so they do not cut across each other and further exclude rough-sleepers

Recommendation 8

DETR and the Home Office should issue joint guidance to police forces, local authorities and voluntary agencies on reducing victimisation, improving services to meet the needs of rough-sleepers as victims and inter-agency working between local community safety partnerships and street homelessness co-ordinating groups.

Recommendation 9

The Home Office should amend its guidance to local community safety partnerships under the Crime and Disorder Act (1998) to designate rough-sleepers as a 'hard-to-reach' group which must be consulted on its community safety needs and have provision made for it within the local strategy.

Reducing offending

Establishing structured intervention and diverting rough-sleepers from offending

Recommendation 10

The Home Office should take the lead, with the support of the Lord Chancellor's Department and DETR, in developing a pilot rough-sleepers' diversion programme which brings together multi-agency services along similar lines to those being applied for Youth Offender Teams.

Providing facilities and support programmes for diverting rough-sleepers

Recommendation 11

Street homeless co-ordinating groups should initiate a joint service review involving police and local service providers which brings forward ways of reducing formal contact between rough-sleepers and police and which looks, in particular, at the provision of day centres; the provision of 24-hour service cover; and, the provision of wet day and night facilities for rough-sleepers.

Recommendation 12

The Department of Health should work in partnership with the Home Office and local street homelessness co-ordinating groups to put in place drug and alcohol detoxification facilities and support programmes as part of a pilot rough-sleepers' diversion from custody programme.

Recommendation 13

Local street homelessness co-ordinating groups, existing service providers and the Department for Employment should review the present extent of self-help provision for rough-sleepers within the local area and bring forward proposals for widening the application of New Deal for Employment opportunities for rough-sleepers.

Targeting and reducing repeat offending by rough-sleepers

Recommendation 14

Local street homelessness co-ordinating groups should work jointly with local community safety partnerships to prepare and include offence reduction plans within local rough-sleeping and community safety strategies.

Identifying the resources to meet the cost of diverting rough-sleepers from offending

Recommendation 15

The Treasury, in partnership with the Home Office, should review current public expenditure arising from street homelessness and crime and bring forward proposals to meet the on-going costs of a diversion from custody programme by re-applying existing resources.

Policing people who sleep rough

Uplifting police participation in partnership

Recommendation 16

DETR and the Home Office should include in their guidance to police forces, local authorities, street homeless co-ordination groups, community safety partnerships and voluntary organisations the requirements for senior police involvement in strategic planning on street homelessness and local connections between community safety and street homelessness strategies.

Widening policing options beyond enforcement

Recommendation 17

Local street homelessness co-ordinating groups should work with local police forces to give priority to improving communication between front-line police officers and outreach teams and to providing one-stop, 24-hour contact points between the services.

Promoting consistency and good practice across police forces

Recommendation 18

All UK police forces should review the policing of street homelessness within the force area and, in particular, their arrangements for strategic partnership on street homelessness; their arrangements for co-ordinating and managing force policy and practice on street homelessness; changes to recording practices on crimes against rough-sleepers; and, the need for officer training.

Recommendation 19

Police and local street homelessness co-ordinating groups, or in their absence, local street homelessness service providers should arrange inter-agency staff training programmes for police officers and outreach staff.

Recommendation 20

The Home Office in partnership with the Association of Chief Police Officers and Police National Training organisations should develop and issue good practice guidance on policing street homelessness.

Connecting social exclusion, street homelessness and crime

Recommendation 21

The Ministerial Committee on Rough-Sleeping, which has responsibility for overseeing the development and delivery of co-ordinated action on rough-sleeping, should review the findings and recommendations from this investigation and bring forward proposals to incorporate them into the Government's action plan for reducing rough-sleeping.

The author acknowledges that responsibility for carrying forward some of the recommendations in Scotland and Wales rests with the Scottish and Welsh executives and agencies within those countries and asks that they are pursued by the appropriate responsible authority.

1. Investigating street homelessness & crime

Introduction

Street homelessness and crime occupy unsettling places in the public mind. Street homelessness is at the same time a picture of personal vulnerability and possible threat. Rough-sleeping is the most visible form of social exclusion; a public portrayal of circumstances which are usually hidden. Crime is a defining mark on the community landscape, a constant thorn which influences people's lives. Both are visible features of UK life in the late 1990s.

Taken together, street homelessness and crime are disquieting, a stark reminder of societal instability and social exclusion. Neither is a recent phenomenon. Both are to some degree products of social change. Both are the recurring object of public concern and public policy. Yet, over the past 30 years, public policy on street homelessness and crime has been largely disconnected and piecemeal.

The history of single homelessness policy over that period is dominated by short-term, ad hoc responses where policy connections have not only been missed but often been in competition. (see Foord, Palmer and Simpson, 1998) A focus upon buildings and provider interests has clashed with the need for diverse facilities and the wishes of rough-sleepers. Social security policy has cut across solutions to help people leave the street and became, in the mid and late 1980s, a major driver of the upward trend in homelessness.

Tackling crime has seen similar disjunction. Rising recorded crime levels and public concern have acted as public policy levers for public order legislation, pushing police towards greater enforcement and giving rise to rapidly growing prison populations, despite growing evidence that prison does not work. Police officers try to reconcile demands for public order policing and greater control over public places with increasing exposure as the 24-hour, 7-day service. Public policy shifts towards care in the community and progressive reductions in other public services have reinforced pressures upon police officers at the sharp end of a front-line service.

When street homelessness and crime come together in the public mind and in public policy it is not surprising that they should reflect the fragmentation and policy competition characteristic of both areas. The public mind is torn between sympathy, giving rise to support for rough-sleepers, and disquiet, giving rise to calls for police enforcement action. Public policy is divided between programmes directed to helping rough-sleepers' leave the street and public order legislation directed at tackling crime and the public's fear of crime which can reinforce the exclusion of people who sleep rough.

Two recent developments offer a possibility of breaking away from past shortcomings. The Government's drive on social exclusion, with its emphasis upon cross-departmental and inter-agency working, has raised street homelessness as a public policy priority. The Social Exclusion Unit's push towards greater local co-ordination on rough-sleeping lays a possible platform to help rough-sleepers move away from the street, sets out to tackle the shortcomings of the Rough-Sleepers' Initiative (RSI), and tries to improve the alignment of Government's five main funding programmes for rough-sleepers. The five main programmes are: The Rough-Sleepers Initiative (DETR); Section 180 Grants (DETR); Resettlement Programme (DSS); Homeless Mentally Ill Initiative (DoH); Drugs and Alcohol Specific Grant (DoH).

Established by the Department of the Environment (DoE) in 1990 and launched initially in London, RSI aimed to render it unnecessary for anyone to sleep rough in central London and in a later phase in other urban areas across the UK. Its focus has been the development of facilities and services to help rough-sleepers settle into permanent housing. RSI evaluations have highlighted the continuing need to improve co-ordination between agencies, and some advances have been made, but an ironic by-product of RSI's emphasis upon competitive service delivery has been fragmentation amongst service providers with a plethora of providers offering similar services to the same clients (see Randall and Brown, 1993, 1996; SEU, 1998).

Fragmentation has been intensified by the lack of alignment between the five main programmes helping rough-sleepers which are run by three different Government Departments, channelled by different routes (some through the local authority, some direct to the voluntary sector) and subject to different rules.

Government has set out its stall on rough-sleeping and social exclusion by expanding DETR's responsibilities beyond housing to include health, access to training, employment and benefits; by setting up a Ministerial Committee to oversee delivery and development of the cross-service action plan; and, by setting a target of reducing rough-sleeping by two-thirds by 2002.

At the same time as the push on rough-sleeping and social exclusion, the Crime and Disorder Act (1998), aims to make communities safer by giving a statutory foundation for community safety partnerships, led by local authorities and police, and supported by a raft of new orders directed at anti-social behaviour, youth offending and drug misuse. The legislation is the enactment of the Government's twin-track policy: tough on crime, tough on the causes of crime.

Rough-sleeping sits at the crossroads of two major Government policies – social exclusion and crime and disorder. It is a litmus test for joined-up government. Is it possible to overcome the fragmentation and policy competition which characterises how we tackle street homelessness and crime? What steps should be taken? How do we make sure that developments on crime and disorder do not cut across work to help rough-sleepers leave the street? Are agencies geared up to deliver by 2002?

More importantly, how should we tackle street homelessness and crime? It lies at the heart of policing and social exclusion, where the social agency tasked with preventing crime and maintaining control over public places comes into contact with the social grouping most visibly excluded from the economic and social mainstream.

Yet, we have little direct information on street homelessness and crime. To connect public policy on social exclusion and crime and disorder we may first have to disconnect street homelessness from crime. To do so we need to investigate and understand what takes place on the street – to map rough-sleepers as victims of crime, as offenders and contact between police and people who are street homeless. This was the purpose of the investigation, the findings of which are reported in the following chapters.

The aims of the investigation

The aims of the investigation were to:

- provide reliable information on the victimisation of people who are street homeless; crimes committed by rough-sleepers; and, the policing of street homelessness;

- identify practical ways of intervening constructively to support rough-sleepers, address their needs and reduce any barriers which victimisation, offending and police contact may put in the way of people leaving the street;
- inform the wider drive to tackle rough-sleepers' social exclusion and identify whether current directions on street homelessness and crime are best suited to achieve the Government's target of reducing rough-sleeping by two-thirds by 2002.

The starting point was information. Too little is known about rough-sleepers' experience as victims of crime and its impact upon their lives. People who are street homeless are not covered by the ongoing sweeps of the British Crime Survey and are therefore excluded from mainstream policy-making on victimisation and crime reduction. No major UK victimisation studies include rough-sleepers. Direct information is limited. Where data exists (see Carlen, 1996) it focuses upon particular aspects of homelessness, such as youth homelessness. It demonstrates the vulnerability of rough-sleepers and highlights the need for further investigation. This study set out to map the nature and extent of victimisation of rough-sleepers; to investigate how rough-sleepers' experiences compare to those of the wider community; to look at whether victimisation is reported; and, to explore fear of crime—whether being on the street gives rise to a higher or lower fear of being a victim of crime (see figure 1.1 for the guiding questions on victimisation).

Figure 1.1 People who sleep rough as victims of crime: guiding questions

- how often are rough-sleepers' victims?
- what kinds of crime do they experience?
- how does this experience (level and type of crime) compare to that of the general population?
- are offences reported?
- how fearful are rough-sleepers of being victims of crime?

More is known about rough-sleepers' offending. This is not surprising. Much of it is likely to take place in public view. Yet, the focus on offending has tended to be narrow and to concentrate upon specific offences, particularly begging (see Murdoch, 1994). This is understandable. Begging and drinking in public places are two recurring public issues connected with street homelessness. But to understand offending and its connection to rough-sleeping we need to go beyond individual offence types and map the nature and extent of offending by people who are street homeless and its likely outcomes. If we are to disconnect street homelessness and offending we need to understand the offences which are being committed, what might give rise to the offending, and whether the offending is unreported, unnoticed or involves police (see figure 1.2 for the guiding questions on offending).

Figure 1.2 Crimes committed by people who sleep rough: guiding questions

- what kinds of crime are committed by people who sleep rough?
- what reasons are given for committing offences?
- are they arrested?
- are they charged?
- how do these crimes compare (in type and level) to those of which they are victims?

Policing street homelessness can be contentious. Some of the recent UK media coverage on 'zero tolerance' policing might lead us to believe that rough-sleeping is the source of criminality and that more robust police action could prevent street homelessness. Kress (1994) documents a growing raft of local bye-laws across the United States criminalising street homelessness, particularly through redefining 'panhandling' or 'begging', and requiring increased police enforcement action to make it stick. There is a need for public discussion on how communities are policed. It is fundamental to policing by consent and it is an ongoing discussion supported by most UK police officers. But we need to understand the connection between street homelessness and crime before we veer off on one particular policing direction. This investigation maps the nature and extent of contact between rough-sleepers and police and sets it in the wider context of how police forces across the UK currently police street homelessness (see figure 1.3 for questions on police contact with rough-sleepers and policing policies, practice and procedures).

No opportunity to make your voice heard and others' unwillingness to listen are common features of social exclusion. This investigation also explored the views of rough-sleepers and police officers on street homelessness and crime and the steps those most immediately involved would like to see taken on victimisation, offending and policing street homelessness.

Figure 1.3 Policing people who sleep rough

Contact between people who sleep rough and the police

- how often do rough-sleepers and police come into contact?
- what kinds of contact take place?
- how satisfied or dissatisfied are rough-sleepers with police contact?
- what actions would rough-sleepers like to see taken to tackle victimisation, reduce offending and improve police contact?

Policing policies and practices

- have forces adopted any particular policing policies, strategies or initiatives for policing street homelessness?
- which policing style, if any, do police forces consider most appropriate and effective for policing people who sleep rough?
- what approaches are employed by police forces towards rough-sleepers as potential victims or offenders?
- what training or guidance, if any, is given to officers who are likely to come into contact with rough-sleepers?
- are there any external influences upon police approaches to street homelessness?
- what multi-agency or partnership initiatives are underway?
- what changes, if any, would police forces like to see in the policing of street homelessness?

The investigation

The investigation had four key elements (see figure 1.4). A *literature and policy review* examined research findings and policy developments on policing, street homelessness and crime in the UK and internationally, particularly in the United States. *Front-line Voluntary Sector Agencies* took part in scoping and sector development sessions in Glasgow, London and Swansea. The scoping sessions explored local and national issues on victimisation, offending and policing street homelessness. The sector development sessions examined local good practice and future tasks which needed to take place in each location to advance work on street homelessness.

Rough-sleepers' victimisation, offending and contact with police were investigated in two ways: by structured group discussions (six discussions, two in each location) and in-depth, one-to-one structured interviews (120 interviews) with rough-sleepers. Rough-sleepers were also asked in both discussion and interview about their view of what needed to be done to tackle street homelessness and crime. Just under one in five (18 per cent) in-depth interviewees were women.

One in five (20 per cent) interviewees were aged 16 to 20 years; two in five (41 per cent) were aged 21 to 29 years; just under one in five (18 per cent) were aged 30 to 39 years; and the remaining one in five (21 per cent) were aged over 40 years. Nearly two in three (63 per cent) interviewees had been street homeless for 24 months or more with the older interviewees, particularly those aged over 50 years having been sleeping rough for many years. One in five (20 per cent) had been street homeless for up to six months. The majority of interviewees were of UK white (80 per cent) or Irish (12 per cent) background. Few (6 per cent) were of African, Asian or Caribbean origin (see Appendix I for further details).

Figure 1.4 Key elements of the investigation

- *Literature and policy review*
- *Front-Line Voluntary Sector Agencies*
  scoping sessions exploring local issues on victimisation, offending and policing street homelessness
  sector development sessions examining local good practice and future tasks
- *Rough-sleepers*
  structured group discussions
  120 in-depth, one-to-one, structured interviews
- *Police*
  survey of all UK police forces on policing policy, practice, local strategy, training, multi-agency work and desired changes in policing street homelessness
  structured group discussions
  one-to-one interviews with senior management, city centre operational management and front-line police officers

Policing street homelessness was investigated in three parts: by a survey of all UK police forces on policing policy, practice, local strategy, training and multi-agency work; through structured group discussions with officers of varying rank (5); and, in one-to-one discussions with senior police management, city centre operational management and front-line police officers (35). The group and one-to-one discussions investigated the extent of victimisation of rough-sleepers, offending and how it impacts policing, the policing of street homelessness and steps which officers would like to see taken to improve the policing of street homelessness and to make officers' work easier and more effective.

Fieldwork took place between May and December 1998 in Glasgow, Swansea and London. The three sites were selected to provide coverage across England, Scotland and Wales; to enable comparison between rough-sleepers' experiences; to provide a broad range of agency and organisation views; and to reflect a potential range of policing styles. Strathclyde Police are pursuing high profile public policing through the 'Spotlight Initiative'; South Wales Police are pursuing community-based policing within Swansea City Centre; and, the Metropolitan Police have developed a range of policing responses, including establishing a specialised street homelessness unit within Charing Cross Division.

A national feedback and discussion seminar was held in November 1998 to consider the initial findings from the investigation and potential priorities for tackling victimisation, reducing offending and developing policing policy and practices.

The remainder of this report sets out the findings from the investigation.

The next chapter explores rough-sleepers as victims of crime. It maps the nature and extent of victimisation experienced by people who sleep rough; analyses the risk of victimisation relative to the wider community; records the extent to which victimisation is reported and unreported to police and the reasons therefore; and, reports on rough-sleepers' fear of crime, how it reflects experiences and expectations. The last section sets out a number of steps to reduce victimisation; increase reporting and tackle fear of crime.

Chapter 3 looks at crimes committed by people who sleep rough. It looks at the offences committed by rough-sleepers and how often they take place; analyses the reasons provided by rough-sleepers to explain why they commit offences; reports on what happens when rough-sleepers offend; and, provides a police assessment of offending by rough-sleepers. The final section sets out the steps to be taken to divert rough-sleepers away from offending whilst at the same time reducing their continuous engagement with the criminal justice system.

Chapter 4 examines how people who sleep rough are policed in the UK. It maps the nature and extent of contact between rough-sleepers and police and reports rough-sleepers' views of police contact.

Thereafter it reviews policing policies, practices and procedures across the UK and sets out officers' views of policing street homelessness. It looks briefly at 'zero tolerance' policing in light of the findings and examines its relevance for policing street homelessness in the UK. It looks at the conflict between rough-sleepers' public lifestyle and the primary police responsibility for policing public places. The last section examines ways of changing contact between rough-sleepers and police, shifting away from an over-reliance upon enforcement and building upon developing good practice across police forces.

Chapter 5 sets out rough-sleepers' and police officers' views on the steps which should be taken to tackle victimisation, reduce offending and improve contact between rough-sleepers and police. It looks briefly at the enduring difficulties arising from drinking in public places. The final section sets out a number of steps to incorporate rough-sleepers' and police officers' wishes into the final recommendations.

In conclusion, the **final chapter** sets out a series of recommendations for tackling victimisation, reducing offending and improving how we police street homelessness.

Appendices provide technical information on the investigation, including a detailed description of the methodology; a listing of figures and tables which appear throughout the report; and, details of the agencies and organisations which took part in or supported the investigation.

2. Rough-sleepers as victims of crime

Introduction

Rough-sleepers' exclusion from the British Crime Survey and other large-scale studies of victimisation highlights their marginal position when it comes to formulating victim policy in the UK. Recent developments have rightly highlighted the importance of victim support in criminal justice. The Crime and Disorder Act (1998) has sought to strengthen services to victims and at the same time afford victims a more central role in the delivery of justice. Street homeless people remain largely beyond such victim support services yet this may offer an initial point of contact or intervention relevant to their needs.

But the importance of criminal victimisation is wider than rough-sleepers' exclusion from victim support services. Being a victim of crime is multiply connected to rough-sleeping and addressing those connections may well be key to tackling street homelessness and helping rough-sleepers make the transition from the streets. A growing body of evidence suggests that criminal victimisation can be a precipitator of street homelessness as well as an inhibitor to leaving the streets once there. Fischer (1992) documents the disproportionate number of rough-sleepers who have been physically or sexually abused before leaving home. Three-fifths of teenagers in a San Francisco study (JAMA, 1988) had been sexually abused before leaving home and half the homeless young people in a New York study (Shaffer and Caton, 1984) reported parental physical abuse which had hospitalised them on at least one occasion before they had run away. More recently, the Social Exclusion Unit (1998) noted the failings of local authority care services and the potential connection between criminal victimisation and the high proportion of young people leaving care who end up sleeping rough in the UK. Much of this criminal victimisation goes unreported.

The part played by criminal victimisation in precipitating homelessness is beyond the scope of this investigation. But it is clear many rough-sleepers may be victims, possibly repeat victims, before they become street homeless and for some, victimisation once on the streets is a continuation of previous experience. This highlights the importance of victim support services as a point of initial contact and intervention for rough-sleepers.

Ironically, the same surveys which exclude rough-sleepers indirectly indicate the potential scale of their victimisation once on the streets. From accumulated sweeps of the British Crime Survey (seven since 1982) we can say with some degree of reliability that crime affects some communities and some sections of communities disproportionately; some individuals suffer repeatedly from crime; fear of crime is more widespread than crime itself, and, the most vulnerable groups are most affected by fear of crime. These would all seem to indicate that rough-sleepers are likely to experience criminal victimisation. What we do not know with any reliability is where the experiences of rough-sleepers fit nor the kinds of support services and policing strategies which are best placed to tackle victimisation and meet rough-sleepers' needs.

This part of the investigation maps the nature and extent of victimisation and draws out implications for how we design services for rough-sleepers, for how we deliver services, and for how agencies work together to reduce victimisation and encourage a transition from the streets. In a later section, we explore the connections between victimisation and offending.

The nature and extent of victimisation

Rough-sleepers' experience of crime is high, often repeated and largely unreported to police. The crimes of which rough-sleepers are victims are more likely to be crimes against the person than property crimes. They reflect the extent to which rough-sleepers live their daily lives in public contact, yet remain separated from the reasonable degree of protection and support which helps sustain the wider population.

Table 2.1 Being a victim of crime

	London		*Swansea*		*Glasgow*		*Total*	
Victim of crime	51	84%	17	57%	26	90%	94	78%
Not a victim of crime	10	16%	13	43%	3	10%	26	22%
Total	61	100%	30	100%	29	100%	120	100%

Nearly four in every five rough-sleepers (78 per cent) had been a victim of crime on at least one occasion during this last period when they had been street homeless (see Table 2.1). The 1998 British Crime

Survey found that 34 per cent of adults in England and Wales had been victims of crime on at least one occasion in the previous year. Even at the broadest level rough-sleepers appear to be more than twice as likely to experience crime than the general population.

But some rough-sleepers may be more vulnerable than others and some areas may be less safe than others. Around 95 per cent of women rough-sleepers had been a victim of crime compared to 75 per cent of men. There may be fewer women rough-sleepers but those who are street homeless appear to be at greater risk than men. Outreach workers in Glasgow and London stressed the additional hardships facing women rough-sleepers and the likelihood that many women may enter prostitution in part because it can help maintain a roof over their heads. Carlen (1996) also found that young homeless women were more likely to be victims of crime than young men. Sixty-five per cent of young women had been a victim at least once compared to 45 per cent of young men.

Swansea appears to be relatively safer for rough-sleepers than Glasgow or London, although it is difficult to determine why that might be. Local agencies and outreach workers have suggested that Swansea has relatively fewer rough-sleepers, many of whom gravitate towards Cardiff and other UK urban centres. It may be a function of city size and the overall number of rough-sleepers. Rough-sleepers in Swansea are also less likely to be victims of verbal abuse and threatening behaviour than street homeless people in London or Glasgow.

Table 2.2 Victims more than once: repeat victimisation
(the percentage of rough-sleepers who had been victims on more than one occasion)

Repeat victim of:	%
Verbal abuse	62
Threat behaviour	53
Common assault	39
Wounding	16
Robbery	22
Theft	42
Extortion	13
Other crime	3

Total number of rough-sleepers = 120

Not only are rough-sleepers more likely to be victims of crime than other citizens they are more likely to be victims more than once and to be victims of crimes against the person (see Tables 2.2 and 2.3). Verbal abuse and threatening behaviour are regular occurrences. They are the backdrop against which street homeless people live. Nearly two in three rough-sleepers (62 per cent) had been verbally abused and over half (53 per cent) threatened with violence more than once. Abusive comments were seen as commonplace, particularly at certain times of the day and from some sections of the public. Later at night was seen to be less safe, particularly when public houses were closing and groups of young males were seen to be most dangerous, not unlike the views of the majority of the population. These were times to be avoided.

Table 2.3 Of which crimes are rough-sleepers' victims?
(the percentage of rough-sleepers who report being victims of crime)

	London	*Swansea*	*Glasgow*	*Total*
Verbal abuse	79	37	62	64
Threat behaviour	54	40	72	55
Common assault	39	33	69	45
Wounding	43	30	24	35
Robbery	25	30	38	29
Theft	57	37	55	52
Extortion	16	13	14	13
Other crime	8	0	10	7

People are victims of more than one type of offence on more than one occasion.

Just over four in ten (42 per cent) had been victims of personal theft more than once, demonstrating the difficulties rough-sleepers have in acquiring or keeping any belongings, however few they might have. The lack of any 'safe' place to leave belongings and their constant exposure to theft are major causes of concern to rough-sleepers. They are constant reminders of their position, in some ways more so than crimes of violence. Repeated personal theft forces rough-sleepers further into daily survival and exclusion. It increases dependence on daily services. When it connects with other problems, such as mental health, drug or alcohol misuse, it makes the possibility of leaving the streets more remote.

Repeat violence is the third feature of personal victimisation. Approximately two in five rough-sleepers (42 per cent) have been assaulted more than once, more than one in five (22 per cent) have been robbed, and one in six (16 per cent) have been wounded more than once. The cost of this level of personal violence is high for both victims and health services. This investigation did not explore the health impact of repeat violence but in a study of the medical records of 340 homeless patients admitted to San Francisco General Hospital in three months in 1983, trauma accounted for one quarter of all homeless admissions. Grenier (1996) found that rough-sleepers were 50 times more likely to die from serious assault than the general population. It is not unreasonable to assume the violent victimisation of rough-sleepers in this study has also placed strain upon the lives of rough-sleepers and emergency demands upon health services.

Some places seem less unsafe than others and to generate slightly different targets for tackling repeat victimisation amongst rough-sleepers. There are three issues which need to be addressed: repeat violence, repeat personal theft and repeat abuse and threatening behaviour. They are a common starting point for tackling victimisation. At the same time there appear to be particular difficulties in different areas. Glasgow may have a difficulty around threatening behaviour, assault and verbal abuse which are experienced by more than three in every five rough-sleepers. London appears to have a high incidence of wounding. Swansea is again less unsafe overall yet it has the same level of extortion from rough-sleepers as the other cities. Whatever the pattern, the message is that we need to tackle repeat victimisation of rough-sleepers and to build it into local crime reduction programmes emerging through the Crime and Disorder Act 1998.

Who offends against rough-sleepers? Some studies (Town and Marchetti, 1984, Solarz, 1986) suggest that rough-sleepers' offending against each other is the most significant source of rough-sleepers' victimisation. This has anecdotal support within police forces and across voluntary agencies where a major source of contact with the police arises from incidents between street homeless people. Small groups of homeless people, particularly those with established alcohol problems, are likely to come to the attention of police through their public activities.

However, this does not mean that other street homeless people are the

Table 2.4 Who commits the offences?
(percentage of different victimisation committed by public and by other rough-sleepers)

	Offender	
	public	rough-sleeper
Verbal abuse	64	36
Threat behaviour	56	44
Common assault	53	47
Wounding	63	38
Robbery	46	53
Theft	50	49
Extortion	50	50
Other crime	88	13

main source of the high levels of victimisation. From police experience it may well be the case that other rough-sleepers are the victimisers in the majority of incidents coming to police attention, particularly if rough-sleepers are unlikely to report their victimisation and police contact is initiated by police presence or by a member of the public. But, rough-sleepers report a different story , as shown in Table 2.4. For them, the general public are a little more dangerous than other rough-sleepers. The general public are often the source of abusive, threatening behaviour and wounding. More surprisingly perhaps, street homeless people appear equally as likely to be stolen from, extorted, robbed and assaulted by members of the public as by other rough-sleepers.

This is not the picture of a largely self-contained grouping which gives rise to most of its own criminal victimisation. It is a picture of a socially excluded group caught in a double bind where people are victimised by the wider general public and other rough-sleepers. If this is the case we require a twin track for tackling victimisation – one which targets ways of reducing victimisation and offending between rough-sleepers but equally as importantly one which targets the general public as perpetrators of a range of offences against rough-sleepers.

At greater risk than others

Within the general population people are at greater risk of being victims of crimes against property than crimes against people or contact crimes as they are labeled in the British Crime Survey. The 1998 British Crime

Survey found the greatest risk of victimisation to be theft from a vehicle. One in ten (ten per cent) households who owned vehicles had something stolen from it in 1997.

The risk of violence is considerably less: fewer than one in 20 adults (4.7 per cent) experienced a violent crime during 1997. This was mostly common assault (3.2 per cent): one in 100 adults (one per cent) was a victim of wounding and fewer than 1 in 100 people (0.8 per cent) were victims of mugging (comprising snatch theft and robbery). The overall likelihood of being a victim of violent crime fell between 1995 and 1997.

Rough-sleepers experience of violent crime is substantially greater. Of rough-sleepers:

- 45 per cent had been victims of assault (almost one in two)
- 35 per cent had been victims of wounding (almost three in five)
- 29 per cent had been victims of robbery (almost one in three)
- 13 per cent had been victims of extortion (just over one in eight)

Overall, rough-sleepers appear to be up to 15 times more likely to experience assault than the wider population and 35 times more likely to be a victim of wounding.

These are average risks and even within vulnerable groups not all risks are equal. The British Crime Survey (1998) found some sections of the community were more likely to be victims of crimes of violence than others. Men were at greater risk than women. People in inner cities at greater risk than people in rural areas. Two sections of the community were at greater risk than others: young men in inner cities, 21 per cent of whom had been a victim of violence and private renters in inner cities of whom 19 per cent had been victims of violence. This throws up two key findings. Rough-sleepers are more than twice as likely to be victims of violence than the highest at risk groups within the wider community. Once they move off the streets, most rough-sleepers will enter the private rented sector in an inner city and will remain within the highest at risk groups. It may be a substantially lower level of risk but it is still markedly higher than the population average and may hinder rough-sleepers' transition into stable accommodation. Constructing places of safety may well require us to pay attention to on-street support; making hostels and first stops safer; and, following through to improve personal safety within some parts of the private rented sector in inner cities. These risks need to be addressed as part of a strategy for reducing victimisation and rough-sleeping and as part of personal community safety strategies in inner city partnerships.

Rough-sleepers are also at greater risk of repeated crimes of violence than the most at risk sections of the general population. Within the general population just under one in 25 women (3.6 per cent) were found to be victims of violence in the 1998 British Crime Survey. Young women were most at risk where just under one in 11 had been victims of violence (8.8 per cent). The majority of this violence is domestic violence. As such it is repeated. 40 per cent of the young women who were victims of violence were victims on more than one occasion. This section is amongst those most at risk of repeated violence within the community.

Nearly one in two women rough-sleepers (47 per cent) had been victims of assault, one in three (33 per cent) a victim of wounding and nearly 2 in 5 victims of robbery (38 per cent). Women rough-sleepers appear to be nearly 12 times more at risk of being assaulted than all crimes of violence against women in the rest of the community. Taken against those women at greatest risk within the general population – young women aged 18 to 24 years – women rough-sleepers are more than five times more likely to be assaulted than all violence against young women. Repeat victimisation is also higher for women rough-sleepers. 90 per cent of women rough-sleepers who had been victims of assault had been victims more than once.

Specific violent crime reduction programmes need to be directed towards rough-sleepers, irrespective of how difficult their construction and delivery might be.

Reporting victimisation – hidden levels of victimisation

Not all crimes are reported. Official crime figures reflect only a proportion of victimisation experienced by the general population. Some sections of the community, often the more vulnerable sections including women and ethnic minority victims, are less likely to report their victimisation.

Street homeless people reported one in five incidents of criminal victimisation (21 per cent). In the British Crime Survey 1998, 44 per cent of victim incidents were reported to police. This may be accounted

Table 2.5 How often is victimisation reported to police?

	London		*Swansea*		*Glasgow*		*Total*	
Reported to Police	13	25%	4	24%	3	12%	20	21%
Not Reported to Police	38	75%	13	76%	23	88%	74	79%
Total	51	100%	17	100%	26	100%	94	100%

for in part by the preponderance of property crimes in the British Crime Survey figures, where a number of victim incidents are reported because they facilitate insurance claims. However, the low reporting level masks the volume of personal crime experienced by rough-sleepers and the frequency with which it occurs.

In keeping with earlier studies (see Farr, Koegel and Burnham, 1986; Stark, 1986 and Huelsman, 1983) serious and violent offences are more likely to be reported to police and multiple victims are more likely to have been in contact with the police on at least one occasion when they had been a victim. One in two wounding victims (50 per cent) and nearly two in five robbery (38 per cent) and assault (37 per cent) victims had reported to police at least once.

Glasgow has a lower level of reporting than London or Swansea. Fewer than one in eight victim incidents were reported to police in Glasgow (12 per cent).

Of those rough-sleepers who had been victims of crime, more than half did not report it because they did not believe it would be taken seriously (56 per cent). One in six (16 per cent) thought the incident was not sufficiently serious to report it, one in seven (14 per cent) were fearful of coming into contact with the police, and one in 12 (eight per cent) were afraid of reprisals if they reported it to the police. The remainder provided other reasons for not reporting (six per cent).

In London, over six in ten victims (62 per cent) believed they would not be taken seriously if they reported an incident. In Glasgow, three in ten (30 per cent) did not report incidents because they were afraid of coming into contact with police. It may be that a number of rough-sleepers in Glasgow had other reasons, such as outstanding warrants, for not wishing to come into police contact. However, that higher fear of police contact in Glasgow, only partly explains the reason why Glasgow has less than half the victim reporting level of London and Swansea.

Overall reporting levels are akin to those found previously amongst other excluded victims. They are similar to the earlier under-reporting of violence against women and racial harassment. Three areas need to be addressed by agencies and the emerging local street homelessness co-ordinating groups:

- how to raise awareness within police forces and other agencies of the extent of criminal victimisation amongst rough-sleepers
- how to redesign services to address the needs of rough-sleepers as victims of crime
- how to tackle the particular issues of a lack of confidence and fear of police contact amongst some victims

Fear of being a victim

Rough-sleepers are not unaware of the dangers of victimisation, particularly violence, which accompany life on the streets. A number of surveys have shown safety to be a high personal priority for rough-sleepers. (see Carlsyn and Moss, 1990; Huelsman, 1983) One outcome of repeated victimisation and concern for personal safety is rough-sleepers' high fears of being a victim of crime. Nearly seven in ten rough-sleepers (69 per cent) stated that they were worried about being a victim of crime. Almost one in three were very worried (30 per cent). This is not unexpected given the risks and reality of victimisation experienced by street homeless people.

Women rough-sleepers are more worried than men, possibly reflecting greater vulnerability and confirming their higher levels of victimisation. More than half women rough-sleepers (53 per cent) were very worried about being a victim of crime and a further one in three were fairly worried (33 per cent). Men rough-sleepers are less fearful than women but they still show levels of fear of crime way above the wider population: two in three men who were sleeping rough reported that they were worried about being a victim of crime (65 per cent) with one in four being very worried (25 per cent).

Fear of crime may also be influenced by the area in which people are sleeping rough, as shown by Table 2.6) Rough-sleepers in Glasgow are most fearful of being a victim. Six out of seven rough-sleepers in

Table 2.6 Fear of being a victim of crime

	London		*Swansea*		*Glasgow*		*Total*	
Very worried	11	18%	13	43%	12	41%	36	30%
Fairly worried	28	46%	6	20%	13	45%	47	39%
Not worried at all	22	36%	11	37%	4	14%	37	31%
Total	61	100%	30	100%	29	100%	120	100%

Glasgow are afraid (86 per cent) whereas just under two in three are afraid in London (64 per cent) and Swansea (63 per cent).

Rough-sleepers' fear of crime appears to differ from the wider population in two significant ways – in the overall level of fear (rough-sleepers are more fearful) and in the crimes which give rise to that fear (rough-sleepers' fear reflects their experiences and is more likely to be fear of personal rather than property crime). In this instance, fear of crime would seem to reflect experience and reality.

Within the general population fear of property crime is more widespread than fear of personal crime. The British Crime Survey (1996) found that 62 per cent of respondents were worried about being a victim of burglary; 44 per cent worried about theft of their car; and 42 per cent worried about theft from their car. Mugging was the most feared crime against the person and was feared by just under half the wider population (47 per cent). Feeling in danger of personal attack was relatively low with just under one in seven (14 per cent) people living in inner city areas being fearful.

Nearly seven in ten rough-sleepers (69 per cent) were afraid of being a victim of crime. The crimes most feared were crimes against the person. Just over half (51 per cent) were worried about being attacked, assaulted or wounded. Theft from the person was not an issue. No rough-sleepers reported theft as the crime which caused greatest concern. Women rough-sleepers were more concerned about being attacked, assaulted or wounded (62 per cent) than men rough-sleepers (48 per cent). Fear of personal violence was the most feared crime in Glasgow, London and Swansea. Fear of being attacked, assaulted or wounded was highest in Glasgow where over seven in ten rough-sleepers (72 per cent) feared these crimes most. London (46 per cent) and Swansea (40 per cent) had slightly lower levels of fear of personal attack but these remain the most feared crimes and are more feared amongst rough-sleepers than the rest of the population.

Next steps

Any debate over whether or not fear of crime accurately reflects experience seems sterile in the face of such high levels of repeat victimisation and crimes against the person. The scale of victimisation and fear of crime is such that it cannot be ignored in any meaningful strategy for providing services which aim to assist rough-sleepers to leave the streets. It would be easy to argue that the quickest way to reduce victimisation of rough-sleepers is to get them off the streets. But this begs three key questions – how safe are the immediate alternatives, particularly hostels which are the most common first step from the streets? what needs to be done now to reduce the victimisation of rough-sleepers for whom leaving the street may be a longer process? Current, pressing needs cannot be set aside whilst other pathways from the street are constructed. It may be that the success of those other pathways depends to some extent upon reducing rough-sleepers' victimisation, particularly for those who may have been on the streets for a long time and whose victimisation has contributed to their further exclusion and lack of trust. Given what appears to be the experience of most rough-sleepers – largely unreported yet high levels of repeated personal crime – where is the incentive to trust the agencies or services which have not taken this as central to their service delivery? Thirdly, what services need to be developed to tackle victimisation and how might we realign existing services so victimisation gets a higher priority?

Personal safety may have taken a backseat to administering to more immediate perceived needs such as food and health. This is understandable yet it may miss an essential component in helping people leave the streets. The scale of victimisation is such that reducing it needs to become a central feature of all services to rough-sleepers and a focal point for co-ordinated services being developed as part of the local strategies to reduce rough-sleeping. At the same time we need to develop specific programmes to reduce repeated crimes of violence against rough-sleepers; increase reporting to police and other agencies; and ensure that hostels and inner-city private rented sector accommodation offers a safer place for rough-sleepers than the streets.

3. Crimes committed by people who sleep rough

Introduction

Rough-sleepers may be excluded from UK victim surveys but they feature more prominently in public perceptions of offending. A series of studies throughout the 1980s highlighted the apparently high rates of criminal activity amongst the street homeless population, particularly men who are sleeping rough (see Fischer, Breakley and Ross, 1989; Holcomb, 1988; McCarthy, 1985). The focus upon arrest rates suggest that rates of arrest in the homeless population exceed expected rates and have consequently helped develop an image of rough-sleepers as frequent offenders. (Crystal and Goldstein, 1984; Rosnow, Shaw and Concord, 1985)

More recently, US and UK debates on 'zero tolerance' of street crime, particularly aggressive begging, have helped fuel the idea of rough-sleepers as threats to public safety and opened up the way for control strategies which try to displace rough-sleepers from public places in a number of ways including bail conditions, CCTV cameras and restrictions upon drinking in public places. Yet little is known about the type of criminal activity which rough-sleepers might engage in or its distribution across the street homeless population.

Being imprisoned or having a prison record is, in itself, not a particularly useful insight into the criminal activities of rough-sleepers. The Social Exclusion Unit (1998) and NACRO (1996) highlighted the high proportion of ex-offenders who become street homeless and the clear conjunction between offending, imprisonment and street homelessness. Many rough-sleepers are ex-offenders. Many ex-offenders end up rough-sleepers. But this tells us little about which might come first – rough-sleeping to prison or prison to rough-sleeping.

Similarly, the serious shortcomings of care in the community policies have not only boosted the number of people with mental health problems coming into contact with the criminal justice system but increased the likelihood that a proportion will have been street homeless at some time in the recent past. In a 1998 study of contact between people with mental health problems and the criminal justice system in North Central London, the Revolving Doors Agency found that 22 per cent of people known to local services had experienced periods of homelessness.

There are clearly overlaps between rough-sleeping, people with mental health problems and ex-offenders. It would be surprising if it were otherwise given the thrust of UK public policy throughout the 1980s and most of the 1990s. But there is a danger, in the absence of an understanding of the extent of victimisation or criminal activity by rough-sleepers, that such overlaps are used to add weight to often anecdotal evidence that street homeless people could be a threat to a safe community.

This is not to excuse criminal activity by people who are street homeless nor to argue that there is no such criminal activity. It is to caution against further excluding rough-sleepers from the social and economic mainstream by labelling them, however conveniently, as potential offenders or threats to community safety, particularly when emerging evidence suggests rough-sleepers experience substantial 'hidden' levels of victimisation and that their offending might not be as publicly threatening as previously portrayed.

In the absence of wider details of the nature and extent of offending by rough-sleepers it is difficult for police and other agencies to develop proactive strategies aimed at reducing offending in the medium to longer term. Agencies are instead pushed towards short-term, reactive responses, often in relative isolation from each other. From a policing perspective problems are 'contained' rather than 'solved' and offending by rough-sleepers enters the recurring nuisance category which requires repeated processing through the criminal justice system with little intervention or possibility of reducing the problem.

The current investigation sought to go beyond an initial assessment of arrest rates to explore the nature and extent of offending by rough-sleepers, the reasons given for offending and the outcomes once rough-sleepers have come into police contact through their offending. At the same time it looked at some local police information on offending which provided a more formal view of contact and offending in Glasgow, Swansea and London.

Nature and extent of offending

Offending by people who sleep rough is high, more often than not repeated, but more likely to arise from personal need than undertaken for personal gain. Rough-sleepers are more likely to be engaged in less serious offences which are not an ongoing threat to the wider public but lead them into regular contact with police. Over four in every five rough-sleepers (85 per cent) reported that they had offended at least once during the last period they were street homeless (see Table 3.1). Offending was highest in Glasgow and London where nine in ten rough-sleepers had offended. Rough-sleepers in Swansea reported less offending, alongside less victimisation, but three in four rough-sleepers (73 per cent) had offended at least once.

Table 3.1 Rough-sleepers as offenders
(the percentage of rough-sleepers who have offended at least once)

	London	*Swansea*	*Glasgow*	*Total*
Offender	89	73	90	85
Non-offender	11	27	10	15

Figures given in percentages

Such high offending rates raise the question of whether street homelessness is, in itself, criminogenic (a situation which is likely to lead to criminal activity). McCarthy and Hagan (1991) in a study of youth homelessness and crime in Toronto conclude that the conditions accompanying street homelessness make it more likely that rough-sleepers will offend. Snow, Baker and Anderson (1989) argue that there are three processes attached to street homelessness which make it more likely that rough-sleepers will offend, namely:

- *the criminalisation of street life* (whereby a number of public activities such as drinking in public places are defined as offences with the consequence that rough-sleepers become frequent offenders either through the public nature of their lives and/or the likelihood that many rough-sleepers have alcohol problems);
- *the stigmatisation of street homelessness* (whereby public concern about rough-sleepers as potential threats to community safety are reflected in closer attention being paid to their behaviour with the consequence that rough-sleepers are processed formally for 'offences' which would otherwise be ignored);

- *the adoption of criminal adaptive behaviour for street survival* (whereby certain offences such as theft from shops or minor public orders offences arise mainly because they are part and parcel of survival on the streets).

Whatever the reasons underpinning offending by rough-sleepers there is no denying the overall scale of offending which rough-sleepers themselves report or the challenge this poses for policing street homelessness and helping rough-sleepers leave the streets. It points up the need for ways of tackling offending which take into account the extent of victimisation and which provide alternatives to processing rough-sleepers continuously through the criminal justice system without intervention.

Table 3.2 Offenders more than once: repeat offending
(percentage of rough-sleepers who had been offenders on more than one occasion)

Repeat offender of:	%
Public Order	53
Theft (Person)	29
Theft (Shop)	57
Theft (from Car)	24
Burglary	23
Robbery	21
Serious Assault	21
Common Assault	38
Other Crime	18

Total number of rough-sleepers = 120

It also highlights the need to understand the kinds of offences being committed and the reasons being given for that offending. This understanding is key to being able to develop tailored crime reduction programmes which may solve the offending rather than managing it as it occurs.

Rough-sleepers are likely to offend more than once and they are more likely to commit offences which are related to their lifestyle (shown in Tables 3.2 and 3.3). The most common offences are theft from shops and minor public order offences, including common assault.

A majority of rough-sleepers had repeatedly stolen from shops

Table 3.3 Being an offender
(the percentage of rough-sleepers who have committed offences at least once)

	London	*Swansea*	*Glasgow*	*Total*
Public order	44	50	76	62
Theft (person)	33	20	45	33
Theft (shop)	67	43	72	63
Theft (from car)	38	17	21	28
Burglary	34	30	14	28
Robbery	28	23	31	27
Serious assault	38	30	34	35
Common assault	46	40	62	48
Other crime	33	13	10	22

People may be offenders on more than one type of offence on more than one occasion.

(57 per cent) or been involved in public order offences (53 per cent). Just as many rough-sleepers had committed assault as had been been victims of assault. Nearly two in five rough-sleepers had committed common assault more than once (38 per cent). Burglary, robbery and serious assault were less common but had still been committed more than once by around one in five rough-sleepers.

Offending falls into two categories:

- *offending which is closely related to rough-sleepers' lives on the street, such as public order, minor assault, theft from shops and personal theft.*
  These offences are committed by a higher proportion of rough-sleepers and are committed more frequently. Nearly two in every three rough-sleepers had stolen from a shop at least once (63 per cent) or committed a public order offence (62 per cent). Nearly one in two rough-sleepers (48 per cent) had committed at least one minor assault.

- *offending which is more serious and less likely to be related to life on the streets, including burglary or theft from cars and crimes against people including serious assault and robbery.*
  These offences are committed by fewer rough-sleepers but those who commit them are likely to have done so more than once.

> Such crimes are committed by fewer than one in three rough-sleepers, but they still constitute a high level of offending for such crimes.

Offending amongst rough-sleepers is high but there would appear to be a smaller core within rough-sleepers who account for the more serious offences. Just as victimisation of rough-sleepers is not equally spread across all rough-sleepers so it would appear that offending, whilst widespread, is best addressed by focussing upon two types of offending. If the aim is to reduce the volume of offending then the target is lifestyle offending such as theft from shops and minor public order offences. If the aim, however, is to reduce serious offending then the target is a smaller grouping within rough-sleepers who account disproportionately for offences such as serious assault, robbery or burglary.

It may be that there is an overlap between this smaller group of offenders and that proportion of victimisation of rough-sleepers which comes from other rough-sleepers. The danger is that an approach which targets all rough-sleepers equally as offenders has two outcomes – it further labels rough-sleepers thereby making it more difficult to provide help to or get assistance from rough-sleepers to reduce crime and it is more likely to focus upon less serious, lifestyle related offending than the smaller core of more serious offenders.

But, how could we focus closely upon the more serious offenders? Two further findings are relevant. More serious offenders are more likely to be men than women and certain offences might be more common in some areas than others.

Women rough-sleepers are equally as likely as men to have committed an offence at least once when they have been sleeping rough. Nearly nine in ten women (85 per cent) report that they have committed an offence. However, they are less likely to have committed more serious offences or to have done so as often. Eight in ten women rough-sleepers (81 per cent) have stolen from shops. Seven in ten (71 per cent) have done so on more than one occasion. Theft from shops is still a common offence amongst men rough-sleepers but less so: 58 per cent of men rough-sleepers have stolen from shops and just over half (54 per cent) have done so more than once.

Women are slightly less likely to have committed minor public order offences or to have done so more than once. Fewer than half women rough-sleepers (43 per cent) had committed a minor public offence more than once compared to more than one in two men (54 per cent). But it is the repetition of serious offences which shows the greatest disparity. Men rough-sleepers are substantially more likely than women to have offended more than once by committing:

- common assault (44 per cent of men; 10 per cent of women)
- serious assault (23 per cent of men; 10 per cent of women)
- burglary (25 per cent of men; 14 per cent of women)

Likewise, the place where people are sleeping rough appears to impact the kinds of offences they commit. Theft from shops is the most common offence in London where two in three rough-sleepers (67 per cent) report they have committed it at least once. Public order (44 per cent) and common assault (46 per cent) are frequent offences but they are reported by fewer than half the people who are street homeless.

In Glasgow, public order offences and common assault vie with theft from shops as the most common offences: three in four rough-sleepers (76 per cent) have committed public order offences; seven in ten (72 per cent) have stolen from shops; and, six in ten (62 per cent) have committed minor assault. Self-reported offending is higher in Glasgow than London or Swansea.

Theft from shops appears less common in Swansea where it has been committed at least once by less than half the rough-sleepers (43 per cent). Public order offences are slightly more common having been committed by one in two rough-sleepers (50 per cent). Swansea experiences the same pattern of offending – public order, assault and theft from shops as the most frequent and fewer more serious offences – as Glasgow and London, but it experiences fewer of them.

There are a number of possible reasons for Swansea's lower levels of victimisation and offending which have been suggested from discussions with outreach workers and police officers. Swansea has fewer rough-sleepers than Glasgow or London. They fall more clearly into two categories: older rough-sleepers, a majority of whom have alcohol related problems and who are known to agencies and a smaller number of younger rough-sleepers who tend to move elsewhere quite rapidly because there are fewer support facilities in Swansea. Fewer rough-sleepers may mean that many are known to police and other agencies.

A throughput for many younger rough-sleepers may mean fewer young street homeless sleeping rough in the City with decreased visibility, less public contact, lower victimisation levels and lower offending.

Whatever the reasons the findings suggest that success in reducing offending amongst rough-sleepers is more likely to be found in focussed programmes which address lifestyle related offending on the one hand and which identify and target a smaller group of more serious offenders on the other. At the same time local community safety and crime reduction strategies need to develop an understanding of local patterns of offending and plan accordingly.

Reasons for offending

Why do rough-sleepers offend? As we discussed earlier, some studies have suggested that street homelessness is accompanied by conditions, such as necessity and stigmatisation, which raise the probability of offending. The findings from this investigation suggest a useful distinction between frequent, lifestyle related offences and a smaller grouping involved in more serious offending. But, what reasons do rough-sleepers give for offending? Factoring rough-sleepers' reasons into crime reduction strategies may make those strategies more likely to succeed.

Rough-sleepers' self-reported reasons for offending support the distinction between lifestyle related offending and more serious offences, although they are quick overall to attribute offending to need rather than intent. Public order offences (79 per cent) and violent offences, such as common assault (84 per cent) and serious assault (74 per cent) are attributed to their situation. Rough-sleepers see such offences as being caused by the circumstances in which they live. Living public lives where violence is a common occurrence, as witnessed by the high levels of victimisation, may raise the likelihood of rough-sleepers acting first rather than awaiting what they see as the inevitable.

Crimes of theft or personal gain are, however, attributed to necessity. Theft from shops (74 per cent), from other people (72 per cent), from cars (61 per cent) and robbery (70 per cent) are seen to arise from need and survival. This is not to say that rough-sleepers agree with such actions or that they believe them to be justified. Time and again, in wider discussions with rough-sleepers, actions such as theft from shops were seen to be a fact of street homeless life if a rough-sleeper were to survive.

It could be argued that a lot of reasoning which lies behind any offending is self-serving. Rough-sleepers may be little different from the rest of the population when it comes to explaining misconduct. Nevertheless, it is worthwhile being able to understand the reasons given for any criminal activity since they can be one key to designing crime reduction strategies which work. Two routes appear fruitful for rough-sleepers – tackling public order and offences of violence by influencing public living and making it safer thereby reducing the need for some of the violence and reducing the need for theft, particularly from shops, by ensuring adequate basic support is accessible. It may not eliminate offending but it could go some way to reducing or containing it.

Outcome of offending by rough-sleepers

What happens when rough-sleepers have offended? Does it give rise to contact with the police or does it largely go unheeded? What happens once police have become involved? There are a number of reasons for asking such questions. It helps establish the extent of formal contact between police and rough-sleepers and it helps map the likely outcomes for rough-sleepers. More importantly, it indicates whether we might be missing an opportunity to intervene to reduce the extent of offending by rough-sleepers and opens the possibility of turning such intervention into a pathway off the streets.

Police involvement is a regular outcome when rough-sleepers offend. No fewer than two in three rough-sleepers who had offended had come into contact with police as a result of their offending. They may not come into police contact every time they offend but the combination of their lives in public places and the level of repeat offending give rise to regular police contact for offending.

Police contact is high across all offences. Nearly 9 in 10 rough-sleepers (87 per cent) who have committed a public order offence report police involvement on at least one occasion. There is little difference between acquisitive crimes, such as theft from a shop (78 per cent) or from another person (72 per cent), and crimes of violence, such as common assault (72 per cent) or serious assault (63 per cent).

When police become involved, formal processing is high. The more serious the offence then the higher the proportion leading to charging and sentencing (see Table 3.4). Most rough-sleepers who have come

Table 3.4 What happens when police become involved?

	No action	*Caution*	*Arrest*	*Charged/ sentenced*
Public Order	8	15	17	60
Theft (Person)	21	0	12	67
Theft (Shop)	5	7	7	80
Theft (from Car)	10	10	10	71
Burglary	8	0	0	92
Robbery	9	0	0	91
Serious Assault	3	3	7	86
Common Assault	12	15	2	71
Other Crime	5	21	11	63

Figures are percentages

into police contact through offending have been formally processed. No fewer than three in five rough-sleepers have been charged and sentenced following police involvement, irrespective of the category of offence.

'No further action' is an unlikely outcome but where it occurs it does so in less serious offences and offences where there may be a lack of evidence or differing accounts of what has taken place. Cautioning is an infrequent outcome, which is unsurprising given the admitted extent of offending and the likelihood that a person will be known to police. Many rough-sleepers will have progressed beyond the point where cautioning is seen by police as a reasonable option, particularly in the absence of any wider intervention, which makes re-offending less likely.

Rough-sleepers are therefore likely to find themselves in regular police contact through offending, particularly minor offending which results in them moving quite rapidly through the limited options for diversion. Add in the possible involvement of alcohol, drug or mental health related difficulties and the absence of workable alternatives and the police find themselves providing a processing service which neither they nor the criminal justice system is designed to deliver.

Police assessments of offending by rough-sleepers

A brief analysis of police statistics paints a similar picture of repeated, low level offending resulting in regular police involvement and a high likelihood of formal processing. Few police forces record offences committed by rough-sleepers as a specific category. Homelessness is most often recorded, where it is recorded at all, under No Fixed Abode (NFA), which usually refers to the fact that police at that time have been unable to obtain a reasonable address for the offender. NFA is therefore likely to include those who are temporarily homeless as well as rough-sleepers. Even fewer police forces specifically record offences where a rough-sleeper is the victim.

This is not surprising. It is too easy to criticise an apparent gap in recording practices, particularly where it might result in problems and policing needs remaining hidden. The issue is what is done about it and how best to go about improving the situation. Police recording is largely driven by Home Office requirements rather than police planning or management needs. This is slowly shifting, partly due to the Crime and Disorder Act (1998) as forces respond to local information requirements arising from community safety audits and strategies.

Outside Home Office requirements, police recording and analysis derives mainly from demands upon police. If a particular problem is identified within an area, from whatever source, then further local information gathering will be undertaken to help define the police response. In practice, this means that already identified problems are more likely to get recurring priority which can, in turn, make it even more difficult for excluded problems to make it onto an already busy agenda.

At the same time, police recording is geared more towards the category of offence than the category of offender. This is understandable. The incident is primary. It is the focal point for investigation and the application of police resources and effort. A category of offender only becomes more important where there is a recurrence of similar offences within an area.

The outcome is twofold: rough-sleepers are more likely to come to police attention as offenders rather than victims *and* recording of incidents involving rough-sleepers is only likely to take place once an ongoing problem has been identified, however that might happen. In the absence of specific guidance to police forces to monitor any connection between street homelessness, victimisation and offending, there are likely to be only a few locally driven initiatives where a particular problem has come to light or captured local attention. It is also more likely, given the exclusion of rough-sleepers, that what will come to light will be partial and focus upon offending rather than the wider picture of victimisation and offending.

Such problems notwithstanding, the three police forces which supported the investigation – Strathclyde, South Wales and the Metropolitan Police – sought to provide what information they could about contact with rough-sleepers.

Glasgow

Strathclyde Police undertook a three-month monitoring programme within the Glasgow City Centre Division which identified incidents involving rough-sleepers as victims and offenders. Over the three months seven crimes were recorded where the victims were street homeless. They were thefts from the person (3), robbery (2) and serious assault (2). During the same period 2,740 persons were arrested, 79 of whom were street homeless (half of one per cent). The offences involved were relatively minor. 28 per cent were public order offences (breach of the peace in Scotland); 24 per cent were outstanding warrants; and 13 per cent were for theft. The remainder were varied but drinking in a public place was the cause of arrest in only 4 per cent of incidents.

There are a number of possibilities why rough-sleepers account for so few recorded arrests in Glasgow. Rough-sleepers in Glasgow could have low levels of contact with police arising from offending, although this is not reflected in self-reports from rough-sleepers. More likely is that the apparently low level comes about because rough-sleepers use addresses of convenience which result in them being no longer classified as NFA or street homeless. Sleeping rough in Glasgow is done out of the public eye. Rough-sleepers indicated that they were unlikely to sleep in doorways or other visible places around the City Centre because it would attract adverse attention. Instead most rough-sleepers engaged in 'skippering' where they would enter derelict or abandoned buildings to sleep. During the day they would 'legitimise' their presence on the street and try to survive by selling the *Big Issue*. Glasgow has a high number of registered sellers of the *Big Issue*. If arrested, rough-sleepers would provide a friend or acquaintance's address in the knowledge that this would assist their release and that it would be accepted by police if it was a reasonable address. For their part, police were willing to accept a friend's or acquaintance's address as being reasonable where the offence was minor. Whatever the reasons, rough-sleepers are not seen by police in Glasgow as a significant source of offending.

Swansea

South Wales Police undertook a six-month analysis of offending in Swansea City Centre. During that period 744 offences were committed for which one or more persons were arrested and charged. Table 3.5 sets out the types of offences and the proportion committed by homeless people. Rough-sleepers in Swansea account for around one in 12 (8 per cent) of all offences in the City Centre for which people have been arrested and charged. The offences are essentially minor and not a threat to the general public, although they take up a recurring proportion of police time.

Table 3.5 Offending in Swansea
(the proportion of offences in Swansea city centre form January to June 1998 for which homeless people were arrested and charged)

	total offences	*% committed by homeless*
Public order	115	3
Drunk & disorderly	143	6
Drunk & incapable	67	26
Breach of the peace	4	0
Theft	170	8
Burglary	21	14
Criminal damage	46	7
Assault	57	2
Warrant	42	14
Drugs	33	3
Section 25	6	0
Total	**744**	**8**

Rough-sleepers account for one in four (26 per cent) incidents where people are drunk and incapable. Rough-sleepers were involved in few public order or assault incidents which are more likely to be seen as a threat by the wider public. Theft, particularly theft from shops, is the single most common offence in Swansea City Centre. Rough-sleepers were arrested and charged for one in 12 of those incidents (8 per cent).

Swansea has few facilities for homeless people. There is one main temporary hostel. South Wales Police also analysed the proportion of offences over the same six-month period for which hostel residents had been arrested and charged. Including temporary hostel residents increased the proportion of total offences to one in nine (11 per cent) from one in 12 (eight per cent). It increased the number of drunk and incapable incidents involving homeless people (both rough-sleepers and temporary hostel residents) by ten; breach of the peace by one; and Section 25 (begging) by one.

It is probable that the public do not differentiate between rough-sleepers and hostel residents. They are more likely to view both as collectively 'homeless'. Taken together rough-sleepers and hostel residents in Swansea do not pose a threat to public order or to community safety. However, given that most of these offences are committed in public view, offending by rough-sleepers and hostel residents, however unthreatening, is the offending most likely to be seen by members of the public. That proximity can, in itself, contribute to an unbalanced perspective on the extent of offending by rough-sleepers.

Similarly, rough-sleepers and hostel residents may be grouped together by police officers. Any distinction is moot when the most common contact is for drunk and incapable or drunk and disorderly. From a policing perspective it is low-level but regular offending; it may not be the most significant source of police concern when compared to late night violence between young people. It is, however, a constant source of that type of offending, drunk and incapable, which many officers believe is better dealt with by social and voluntary services rather than police.

London

The Metropolitan Police (Charing Cross Division) provided access to a homeless and begging arrest trend analysis for the 12-month period from September 1997 to August 1998. Charing Cross Division polices central London including Trafalgar Square, Covent Garden and Piccadilly. The Division hosts the only dedicated street homelessness policing unit in a UK police force. The Division has the highest concentration of rough-sleepers in London. According to police, on any given night, there may be upwards of 200 people sleeping rough across the Division. The scale of rough-sleeping is one of the largest policing issues for the Division.

A total of 8,540 arrests were made within the Charing Cross Division during the 12 month period. Of those 899 arrests were made for begging and 2,029 homeless people were arrested in connection with incidents. Homeless people accounted for nearly one in four people arrested within the Division over the 12 months (24 per cent). Three in four homeless people (75 per cent) were arrested for minor offences: begging (34 per cent); drunkenness (31 per cent); other minor offences (14 per cent).

Homeless people were half as likely to be arrested for serious offences as other suspects. One in five homeless people (21 per cent) was arrested for more serious criminal matters including drugs (three per cent), burglary (one per cent), vehicle crime (three per cent). More than two in five arrests of non-homeless people (43 per cent) were in connection with serious criminal incidents.

Table 3.6 Main disposals of cases in which homeless persons and people begging were arrested
(Charing Cross Division, Metropolitan Police, September 1997 to August 1998)

	Homeless	*Begging*	*All arrests*
Charged	28	37	27
Cautioned/Warned	47	63	40
Bailed to return	4	0	19
No further action	4	0	5

Source: Homeless and begging trend analysis, Charing Cross Division, Metropolitan Police

At the same time, a larger than average proportion of street homeless people arrested and people arrested for begging were formally processed and charged, cautioned or warned (see Table 3.6). Few homeless people or those arrested for begging were bailed to return. Nearly one in five (19 per cent) of all people arrested were bailed to return. In contrast one in 25 (four per cent) of rough-sleepers who were arrested were bailed to return and no-one who was arrested for begging was bailed to return. Formal processing appears to be the main option in the absence of diversion programmes. Being bailed to return is not a viable option where there is no reasonable address.

Begging

Begging is a difficult issue for both rough-sleepers and the general public. It is cited by police as the most frequent source of public complaint connected to homeless people, and by rough-sleepers as a regular source of contact with police. From police figures it was not a significant source of arrest in Glasgow or Swansea. This is not the case in central London.

One in ten arrests within Charing Cross Division (ten per cent) during the 12-month period was for begging. But, not all those arrested for begging were street homeless. Just less than one quarter of those arrested for begging (24 per cent) had a fixed abode and were not homeless. Police report that this is a slight increase of one per cent over the previous reporting period.

Everyone arrested for begging was formally processed: two in three were cautioned or warned (63 per cent) with the remaining one in three (37 per cent) being charged. Police officers advise that arrest is reached after a person has been informally warned about begging; 80 per cent of those arrested for begging during the 12 months were arrested once only. There is, however, a smaller group of one in five arrests where the person has been arrested more than once within the 12 months. Around one in 100 (one per cent) persons arrested for begging were persistent offenders who had been arrested on more than ten occasions over the previous year.

From police assessments, offending by rough-sleepers is predominantly minor; most often arising from alcohol or public order offences; a small, but constant proportion of overall offending; requiring a regular commitment of police time and resources; and, leading to formal processing once arrested.

Next steps

Rough-sleepers offend frequently and get formally processed frequently. There is little intervention, although there is a need for it. Rough-sleepers are not a predatory threat to the wider community. Rough-sleepers are more likely to be on the receiving end of crimes against the person from the general public than they are to commit crimes of violence against the general public. This is not to say that some rough-sleepers may not appear threatening or that the combination of alcohol-related offending and rough-sleepers' public lives does not give rise to increased public concern. It means there is a distinction between perception and reality.

In police terms, rough-sleepers are not major offenders. They do not account for the majority of crime and their offending is low level. But it is persistent and recurring and in the absence of any ways of diverting rough-sleepers or breaking the cycle of offending, rough-sleepers take up police time and resources. A significant proportion of arrests arise from alcohol misuse. A rising number are linked to drug misuse. The absence of detoxification facilities is a major barrier to rough-sleepers and police alike.

A number of tasks need to be undertaken if we are to successfully reduce offending by rough-sleepers; reduce the proportion of rough-sleepers being formally processed for repeat minor offences; and, release police resources to concentrate upon more serious offending outwith people who are street homeless. The key to reducing offending and the key to helping rough-sleepers to leave the streets is structured intervention at those points where it is most likely to be heeded, be needed and to have an impact. Offending, however minor, is an opportunity for structured intervention which is currently being missed.

Instead, police forces and the criminal justice system are being asked to deliver care and social service solutions which they are not equipped to provide. Intervention and diversion from custody, or even from the later stages of processing through the system, is not commonplace. The Crime and Disorder Act (1998) is trying to shift the criminal justice balance away from unproductive, costly processing and imprisonment towards rehabilitation and, in some instances, restoration. It is a step in the right direction. Yet, there is little evidence so far that the multi-agency services needed to underpin that shift, particularly for rough-sleepers, are developing at the speed needed to make a meaningful difference.

Moves toward better co-ordination of services for rough-sleepers are a first step to reducing offending but diversion programmes should be increased if there is to be any likelihood of breaking the offending cycle and meeting the 2002 targets for helping people leave the streets.

4. Policing people who sleep rough

Introduction

Recent US and UK debates about 'zero tolerance' of crime, particularly street crime, have focused fresh attention upon the policing of public areas and, not surprisingly, their most visible residents, rough-sleepers. This is not new. Vagrancy and public order have gone hand-in-hand with perceived fears for public safety for centuries (see Chambliss, 1964; Barak, 1987; Barak and Bohm, 1989; Aulette and Aulette, 1987). Organised policing in the UK owes its genesis in no small part to such public concerns. The recurring emphasis upon public order policing and its centrality in UK policing reflect this history.

Yet, fears about vagrancy and public order can be inaccurate and misleading. The previous sections on victimisation and offending support the view that rough-sleepers experience hidden levels of victimisation and are not a predatory threat to community safety. People who sleep rough may come into frequent contact with police and require the continual application of police resources, but the offending is mainly low level and a public nuisance rather than a public threat.

This does not mean that rough-sleepers do not offend; that their public lifestyle is not seen as threatening by some sections of the public; nor, that people who sleep rough should not be policed. These are all legitimate considerations. But it raises questions about how best to police rough-sleepers and whether one policing policy or style, for example 'zero tolerance', is likely to be more or less effective than another. It also raises questions about what we are seeking to achieve when policing people who sleep rough.

Running alongside the debate on 'zero tolerance' policing in the UK has been another national debate of particular importance for rough-sleepers – tackling social exclusion. Street homelessness is the most publicly visible manifestation of social exclusion and a reduction of two-thirds by 2002 is a specified measure of the success of the Government's strategy (SEU, 1998).

Policing policies and practices can help or hinder the social inclusion of rough-sleepers. For example, in the absence of any meaningful intervention for rough-sleepers within the criminal justice system, policing policies and practices that lead to increased formal contact between rough-sleepers and the criminal justice system simply increase the amount of 'churning' taking place within the system. This exacerbates rough-sleepers' social exclusion and makes it more difficult to leave the streets. In contrast, work between South Wales Police and the *Big Issue* Cymru in Swansea, where patrol officers report vendors' infringements of their code of conduct through a liaison officer, are helping police the City Centre with less recourse to formal processing.

However, before we can explore what 'zero tolerance' or any other style of policing might mean for rough-sleepers we need to be able to map contact between rough-sleepers and the police and to examine how UK police forces police street homelessness. This part of the investigation looks at the nature and extent of contact between rough-sleepers and the police and sets out the views of people who sleep rough on their contact with police. It also reviews policing policies and practices on street homelessness across UK police forces and reports the views of police officers on their contact with people who sleep rough.

Contact between people who sleep rough and the police

People who sleep rough are in regular, repeated contact with police over and above their high levels of contact which arise through low-level offending. Police contact, initiated mainly by police as part of their daily policing, is a significant feature of the lives of rough-sleepers. Almost nine in ten rough-sleepers (87 per cent) had contact with police during the last period of street homelessness (see Table 4.1). Contact with police, for whatever reason, is one of the more regular connections between people who sleep rough and wider society. This is not particularly surprising given rough-sleepers' public lifestyle and police responsibility for policing public spaces. However, the nature of that

Table 4.1 Contact between rough sleepers and police (percentage of rough-sleepers who have had contact with police during last period when street homeless)

	London		*Swansea*		*Glasgow*		*Total*	
Contact with police	57	93%	22	73%	26	90%	105	87%
No contact with police	4	7%	8	27%	3	10%	15	13%
Total	61	100%	30	100%	29	100%	120	100%

Table 4.2 What kind of regular contact?
(the percentage of rough-sleepers experiencing different sources of police contact)

	London	*Swansea*	*Glasgow*	*Total*
Begging	54	17	55	45
Selling *Big Issue*	11	0	38	15
Public drinking	64	40	24	48
Asleep (day)	51	33	31	42
Asleep (night)	57	30	52	49
Involved in incident	74	47	34	58
Needing assistance	41	10	10	26
Police patrolling	84	37	76	70
Other contact	3	3	21	8

regular contact may carry disproportionate importance for rough-sleepers' views of their relations with the wider world. It certainly influences how they live their lives. The question is the direction the influence takes and the extent to which police are able to play a constructive part in helping rough-sleepers move from the streets.

Rough-sleepers in London (93 per cent) and Glasgow (90 per cent) are more likely to have had police contact than rough-sleepers in Swansea (73 per cent). This may be due, in part, to the length of the last period of rough-sleeping. People who sleep rough in Swansea tend to be younger and to have spent a shorter period on the streets. But, it also reflects the high levels of formal police contact arising when rough-sleepers have offended. Police contact with rough-sleepers appears to be more formal than informal. It is more likely to be initiated by police than by rough-sleepers. Table 4.2 sets out the range of regular contact; Table 4.3 sets out weekly contact.

Police responsibilities for policing public areas and rough-sleepers' lifestyles are the two main sources for contact: seven in ten rough-sleepers (70 per cent) have come into contact with police whilst police have been carrying out patrols and more than one in two (58 per cent) have had contact arising from their involvement in an incident. This is contact during formal police functions.

Similarly, rough-sleepers' lifestyle plays a large part in police contact. Almost one in two (48 per cent) had police contact whilst drinking in a public place and more than two in five (45 per cent) whilst begging.

Table 4.3 Contact more than once: repeat police contact
(the percentage of rough-sleepers who had police contact at least weekly)

Repeat contact while:	%
Begging	33
Selling *Big Issue*	10
Public drinking	32
Asleep (day)	28
Asleep (night)	30
Involved in incident	12
Needing assistance	4
Police patrolling	53
Other contact	4

Total number of rough-sleepers:120

Sleeping in public also attracts police attention whether by day (42 per cent) or by night (49 per cent). The three participating police forces (Glasgow, London and Swansea) all reported that they would expect a police officer to check the welfare of a majority of persons found sleeping in public by day or night. Contact whilst needing assistance (26 per cent) or whilst taking part in self-help work, such as selling the *Big Issue* (15 per cent), is less likely to be a source of contact with police.

The kind of regular contact between police and rough-sleepers varies in different locations but the police remain more likely to be the initiators of contact and for that contact to be formal (see Table 4.1). Multiple contact between police and rough-sleepers in London is high. This may reflect the work of the street homeless unit as a specific policing initiative and in raising general awareness across officers. It may also reflect the number of rough-sleepers in central London. More than eight in ten (84 per cent) rough-sleepers in London have had police contact whilst police are on patrol. Involvement in an incident (74 per cent), public drinking (64 per cent) and begging (54 per cent) are all major sources of police contact in London. Police in London are approached more frequently by rough-sleepers when they require assistance. Over two in five (41 per cent) of people sleeping rough had been in police contact when they needed assistance. This is four times greater than in Swansea or Glasgow.

Public drinking is less likely to be the source of contact between rough-sleepers and police in Glasgow than elsewhere. Fewer than one in four (24 per cent) rough-sleepers in Glasgow had come into contact with police whilst drinking in a public place. Glasgow operates a widespread ban on all drinking in public places. The primary aim has been to reduce the level of street violence, particularly amongst young men in the City Centre, by reducing the availability of alcohol and glass containers. A by-product would appear to be a reduction in contact between rough-sleepers and police over drinking in public places. Given the overlap between rough-sleeping and problems with alcohol it is unlikely that people who sleep rough are drinking less. It is more probable that drinking continues outside the public eye and that rough-sleepers have sought out derelict buildings and similar places. It may also account in part for the infrequency (one in ten) of contact whilst needing assistance. A difficult trade off may be taking place. An improvement in public safety by controlling public drinking and reducing drink related violence may be pushing rough-sleepers out of public view, increasing their exclusion and placing them at greater risk. It is difficult to discern whether such a process is underway because victimisation levels are already obscured by significant under-reporting. Yet, it needs to be borne in mind when we come to design and deliver effective victim support services.

Selling the Big Issue

Big Issue vendors in Glasgow are more likely to come into contact with police when selling the paper than in London or Swansea. Nearly two in five (38 per cent) rough-sleepers in Glasgow have come into police contact while selling the *Big Issue*. This is not a significant source of police contact in London (11 per cent) or Swansea (none). At the time of the investigation there had been a gap in liaison between police and the *Big Issue* in Glasgow. Earlier liaison effectively ended when the police officer involved transferred to another post. A combination of little liaison and a police view, rightly or wrongly, that a significant number of registered vendors are not street homeless appears to have led to a high level of contact between police and vendors relative to other locations. The high incidence of low level offending by rough-sleepers and their irregular lifestyle ensures that at any time a proportion will have outstanding warrants for failure to appear at court and similar matters. This reinforces the police view of rough-sleepers as offenders and substantiates further contact with vendors. From a rough-sleepers' perspective, registration for the *Big Issue* provides access to income and legitimises their presence on the street. A *Big Issue* vendor's badge is a desirable acquisition for rough-sleepers.

In comparison there is little formal contact between police and *Big Issue* vendors in Swansea. This was not always the case. Vendors reported regular contact when the *Big Issue* first appeared on the streets. Similarly, police reported a number of incidents involving *Big Issue* vendors, including a public incident involving a vendor's dog and a guide dog for the blind which caused local concern. Two actions had been taken. A community constable was assigned to permanent duty within the pedestrianised City Centre and a community liaison sergeant at Divisional headquarters established an agreed liaison procedure with the *Big Issue*. Any infringements of the *Big Issue* code of conduct observed by police officers are reported to the *Big Issue* via the liaison sergeant. Police believe this has reduced the need for formal intervention and provided a policing option other than enforcement.

This may also have influenced the frequency of contact between police and rough-sleepers whilst police are on patrol in Swansea. Just over one in three (37 per cent) rough-sleepers in Swansea report contact with police on patrol. This is less than half the contact level in Glasgow (76 per cent) and London (84 per cent). This may be a double-edged sword. The overall contact level through patrol is reduced yet the majority of contact remains formal. It may have the benefit for police and rough-sleepers that it lessens the frequency of contact and the likelihood that patrol contact might develop into an incident. But it also ensures that the majority contact is formal and incident related. The largest single source of contact between rough-sleepers and police in Swansea takes place during an incident (47 per cent).

The overall pattern of regular contact is formal and self-reinforcing. Offending or the expectation of offending is the starting point for most contact between rough-sleepers and police. It is more likely to be formal contact, initiated by police and relating to incidents or lifestyle behaviour which is seen to be publicly difficult. Rough-sleepers are less likely to initiate contact, even when needing assistance. From a police perspective, contact arises as part of regular public policing and although police initiate a majority of the contact, it is contact directly related to policing the area. When police come into contact with rough-sleepers it is likely to have arisen, from a police perspective, because it requires to be policed, albeit at a fairly low level. It is not because police are necessarily going out to look for people who sleep rough. It is more that they live in the public sphere and are recognised by police as a source of regular, low level incidents.

Yet, this poses two challenges. It is not an unreasonable perspective, but it is unbalanced. It omits hidden levels of unreported victimisation not dissimilar to the way in which policing previously overlooked the scale of racial harassment and violence against women. Secondly, if the pattern of formal contact continues to dominate contact between rough-sleepers and police, rough-sleepers are likely to continue to be repeatedly processed for low-level offending. This reinforces rather than reduces social exclusion. It does not break or intervene in the 'offending-formal processing-street homeless' cycle which sits at the heart of the social exclusion of rough-sleepers and governs contact between police and people who sleep rough.

But police are unable to solve these challenges on their own. The present dominant cycle of formal processing stems in part from police being asked to deliver social services they are not in a position to deliver. In the absence of intervention and diversion options and confronted with a perspective which emphasises offending it is not surprising that police are more likely to follow an enforcement route when dealing with rough-sleepers.

From a rough-sleepers' perspective contact with police is regular and frequently formal. It comes through their minor offending or their public life on the streets. It ignores or sets aside their victimisation and the accompanying sense of injustice and exclusion. It may, on occasion, be supportive (for example, checking welfare whilst asleep or while needing assistance) but it is largely police initiated and related to governing their behaviour (begging or drinking in public). It is a common occurrence and a fact of life on the streets but it leads nowhere except custody.

Rough-sleepers' views of police contact

Not surprisingly, given the frequency with which it leads to formal processing or arises from their lifestyle, rough-sleepers have a dim view of their contact with police (see Table 4.4). A majority of rough-sleepers

Table 4.4 Rough-sleepers' satisfaction or dissatisfaction with police contact

	London	*Swansea*	*Glasgow*	*Total*
Very Satisfied	17	5	0	10
Fairly Satisfied	16	5	8	11
Neither	29	9	15	22
Fairly Dissatisfied	14	18	15	15
Very Dissatisfied	24	64	62	42

Figures given in percentages

(57 per cent) are very or fairly dissatisfied with their contact with police. Dissatisfaction is highest in Swansea (82 per cent) and Glasgow (77 per cent) and stems mainly from being stopped and questioned or being moved on by officers.

Rough-sleepers in London are less badly disposed towards their contact with police. One in three (33 per cent) people who sleep rough in London report they are satisfied with their police contact. Satisfaction arises from officers providing assistance and a secure outcome from an incident. A greater proportion (38 per cent) are dissatisfied but London is the only location where a majority of rough-sleepers are not negative towards police contact. London is also the only location where a significant proportion of rough-sleepers (41 per cent) report contact with the police when they required assistance. Four times as many rough-sleepers in London report assistance contact with police than in Glasgow or Swansea (see Table 4.2).

It seems fairly straightforward. Formal, police initiated contact is judged more negatively than rough-sleeper initiated assistance contact. A number of outcomes appear likely where formal, police initiated contact dominates relations between rough-sleepers and police and where victim levels remain hidden:

- rough-sleepers' offending is likely to dominate how they are policed
- rough-sleepers are likely to continue to be processed frequently without intervention or diversion
- the police and the criminal justice system will continue to be asked to deliver social outcomes without the wherewithal or support to do so

- rough-sleepers' dissatisfaction with police contact will remain high, unless there is a growth in police assistance contact
- in the absence of wider options police will be constantly pushed towards enforcement policing as the traditional, defensive policing style

Police may continue to seek to contain and manage street homelessness through the restricted options they have available but are unlikely to be able to break through and resolve the wider problems associated with policing street homelessness. Police resources will continue to be taken up with enforcement policing for street homelessness, dealing with regular, minor, nuisance offending. For rough-sleepers the outcome is equally unrewarding – a major connection to the wider society which focuses upon their offending, processes them regularly without intervention and extends their social exclusion.

The challenge is how we might break free from a cycle of contact which benefits neither police nor rough-sleepers. The solution does not appear to lie within policing policies or practices which are narrowly offender focused. This is not to say that rough-sleepers should not be formally policed when they have committed an offence. Rather it is to recognise that this alone is a short-term policing response which will contain or manage the individual incident without resolving the ongoing victimisation or offending. A substantial element of policing any situation requires a balance between policing individual incidents and seeking to influence any recurring pattern. To contribute constructively to tackling social exclusion and reducing both victimisation and offending in the medium to longer term would appear to require a wider set of policing options than the offender based policing which currently dominates contact between rough-sleepers and police.

But how do UK police forces currently police street homelessness? The nature and extent of contact between police and rough-sleepers indicates that it is essentially formal, offence derived, arising from behaviour in public places and directed towards the individual incident. How is this reflected, if at all, in policing policies and priorities on street homelessness? And, how do police officers' view the policing of rough-sleeping?

Policing street homelessness: UK policing policies and practices

For three out of four (75 per cent) UK police forces street homelessness is not seen as a significant policing issue within the area. With few exceptions, mainly in south and south-west England, rural forces are less likely to report rough-sleeping as a local policing issue. Rural police forces are aware of a small number of people sleeping rough within their area, often having slept rough for a long period, but in policing terms overall numbers are few and policing requirements are minimal in comparison to other local policing issues. The scale of homelessness in rural areas may be under-estimated but it does not appear to attract or require regular police attention or resources.

From a policing perspective, policing rough-sleeping is largely an urban and metropolitan matter and even within a force area street homelessness is likely to be visibly concentrated within a few localities, particularly town and city centres. This has implications for how street homelessness is policed. In the grand policing scheme street homelessness is not a major policing issue across the UK. Relatively few police officers will have regular, direct experience of policing rough-sleeping. Even within an urban or metropolitan police force, experience of regular, direct policing of street homelessness is likely to be restricted to officers working in relatively few areas. In some instances this may be restricted to fairly few community and beat constables whose local area of responsibility includes places where rough-sleepers gather at night or during the day.

Add to this the seemingly intractable nature of policing rough-sleeping and the lack of wider policing options and it is not surprising that the official view of the police role in tackling rough-sleeping is narrowly defined. Insofar as there is a single official policing policy on policing homelessness in the UK it can be summarised as follows:

> The police service is responsible for providing a wide range of services to the public, central to which is the fight against crime. It aims to treat all members of the public fairly, without prejudice or discrimination on any improper ground. The primary involvement of the police with the homeless will therefore, as with all other members of society, be with those who are either the victims or perpetrators of crime.
>
> *RSI: The Next Challenge* Department of the Environment 1996 p25

Table 4.5 Policing street homelessness: UK policing policies and practices

Force policies or strategies on street homelessness		
No specific policy or strategy	35	78%
Specific policies or strategies:		
Rough-Sleeping Initiative derived	3	7%
Force Equality Statement derived	3	7%
Policy on begging	3	7%
Force Order on Destitution	1	2%*
Key issues in policing street homelessness (Multiple responses)		
None	19	33%
Begging	9	16%
Public drunkenness	6	10%
Overlap of drug and alcohol problems	1	2%
Mental health-related problems	3	5%
Accommodation shortage	7	12%
Onward referral by police	13	22%
Force training on policing street homelessness		
No specific training	35	78%
Training through probationer training	4	9%
Procedural guidelines or equality training	2	4%
Specialised training (inc mental health)	3	7%
Specific on the job training	1	2%
Influences upon policing street homelessness		
None	29	64%
Retailers	8	18%
Local authorities	5	11%
Street homeless agencies/shelters/hostels	2	4%
Media	1	2%*
Multi-agency partnerships/initiatives		
None	18	40%
Rough-sleepers initiative related	5	11%
Informal liaison/Working with other services	18	40%
Funding bid driven	2	4%
City Management Partnership	2	4%*

Forces responding: 45

**Percentage totals may be more or less than 100% due to rounding figures*

But we know that victimisation is largely unreported and difficult to police in the absence of any victim support programmes for rough-sleepers. Policing street homelessness from a crime fighting standpoint focuses upon offending. Individualise the policing response in this context by pushing responsibility on to individual officers because it is not a UK or force-wide policing issue and two outcomes are likely – the policing of rough-sleepers effectively starts and finishes with their offending and police remain locked into an unproductive process.

With few exceptions, policing street homelessness is not a policing priority in the UK. Few police forces have adopted specific force policies or strategies; initiated or provided officer training or become involved in multi-agency partnerships. (see Table 4.5) Just over one in five (23 per cent) forces report a force policy or strategy which deals with rough-sleeping. Those policies derive from police involvement in the rough-sleeping initiative (where police have adopted the local RSI strategy as their own guide); from the force equality statement (which reflects the force commitment to act impartially and without discrimination in delivering services); and, in response to begging in public places. One force has a specific force order on policing destitution which guides officers' actions on rough-sleeping. Nearly four in five (78 per cent) forces have no specific policy or strategy on street homelessness. The expectation is that officers will act impartially when dealing with issues arising from street homelessness as they take place.

Where policing rough-sleeping is a policing priority the police role is divided between responding to problems associated with street homelessness and referring rough-sleepers onward to other agencies. One in three (33 per cent) forces see a combination of begging, public drunkenness, mental health and an overlap between alcohol and drug misuse as key issues in policing street homelessness. A further one in three (34 per cent) forces see the time spent referring rough-sleepers to other agencies and a local shortage of accommodation as central to policing rough-sleepers. With the possible exception of additional accommodation these are essentially problem management rather than problem-solving responses.

Where street homelessness is seen to be a policing issue, mainly because there are higher numbers of street homeless people or there is a perceived public nuisance, the primary policing response is driven by offending and criminal incident rather than victimisation. Three broad policing styles appear to dominate:

- *enforcement policing* (Where rough-sleeping is picked up as a result of the public nature of offending and policed to influence the public presence and behaviour of rough-sleepers by tackling begging, drinking in public places, moving people on and on occasion seeking bail conditions to exclude rough-sleepers from particular public areas. The focus is to reduce offending in public, however minor, and the outcome is a higher rate of formal processing through the criminal justice system.)
- *supportive, graded policing* (Where officers provide advice on support services and onward referral rather than formal processing. Public activities amongst rough-sleepers and between rough-sleepers and the general public are regulated by informal and formal cautioning rather than automatic arrest. Several forces operate a graded response to begging applying cautioning as a means of establishing working contact with rough-sleepers before proceeding to arrest if the behaviour continues. Other forces appear less tolerant of begging and proceed rapidly to arrest accompanied by bail conditions excluding rough-sleepers from central areas and reducing the likelihood of public contact.)
- *individualised policing* (Where community and beat officers are expected to take local responsibility for managing, containing and reducing any policing issues within their area arising from rough-sleeping. This is a more common policing response in areas where street homelessness is long established yet relatively small in scale. In effect a local accommodation is reached about behaviour deemed acceptable and unacceptable. It is still offence and behaviour driven and aimed at managing crime rather than solving recurring problems.)

Most forces (64 per cent) report no external local influences upon policing street homelessness principally because rough-sleeping is not seen to be a local issue. However, where street homelessness exists and police see it as a policing issue, forces report some external pressure from retailers (18 per cent) and local authorities, particularly town centre management (11 per cent). Pressure from these sources tries to gain police enforcement action against rough-sleepers mainly to move the issue elsewhere and out of the public eye. Only one force regards media pressure as influencing the policing of street homelessness. Few forces (four per cent) feel under pressure from homelessness agencies to police rough-sleeping differently from current practice.

Few forces provide specific training on street homelessness (22 per cent). Much of the training is contained within broader programmes such as probationer training (nine per cent) or personal skills/equality training (four per cent) and a growing proportion arises from specialised training on mental health (seven per cent). One force has specific on the job training for officers working in the area with the highest number of rough-sleepers. Forces may have under-reported the level of informal training and guidance which takes place often at divisional or station level but it appears that most officers' experience of policing street homelessness takes place through being posted to an area where rough-sleepers gather.

Multi-agency partnerships

Multi-agency partnerships or initiatives on street homelessness are on the increase. Three in five forces (60 per cent) are involved, however slightly, in partnership work, but the majority of this involvement (40 per cent) remains informal and largely unstructured. Officers at all ranks reported that liaison with other services was more likely to come from personal contacts rather than through a structured, regular meeting with other agencies. This may be set to change with the ongoing development of local community safety partnerships arising out of the Crime and Disorder Act (1998) and Government proposals to appoint local street homelessness co-ordinators as part of the drive to reduce social exclusion.

Just over one in ten (11 per cent) forces report an involvement in the Rough-Sleepers' Initiative, but in many areas, police appear to play an indirect part in the Initiative, often being represented at a junior level and engaging only when crime related issues are being discussed. Recent developments on Crime and Disorder partnerships and street homelessness co-ordination are an opportunity for police to broaden the options for policing street homelessness and to break free of the present cycle. To take advantage of this opportunity police forces need to review their current policing of street homelessness; take the management, structural and training steps required to shift away from an offence driven to a problem-solving policing approach; and, overhaul and upgrade police involvement in multi-agency partnerships which can play a part in tackling street homelessness. In the latter instance, police involvement is needed at both strategic and service delivery levels.

Policing is not peripheral to street homelessness. It may be unable to 'solve' rough-sleeping, that is outwith the purpose and scope of policing alone, but it has substantial influence upon life on the streets and a greater contribution to make than managing offending in public which is its present dominant function. Likewise, street homelessness partnerships and local community safety partnerships are likely to find it difficult to reduce rough-sleeping without a police involvement which goes beyond enforcement. Whilst the provision of appropriate local accommodation, support services and pathways from the streets are important for reducing rough-sleeping they will be inhibited, if not undermined, by a policing style which is narrowly focused on offending without intervention.

The overall picture is that policing rough-sleeping has a low policing profile except in a few localised areas. Consequently police forces outside those areas have little experience of policing street homelessness. Within those areas, experience is concentrated amongst relatively few officers who receive little specific guidance or training other than the expectation that they will respond to and manage policing difficulties within their area. Where there are external influences upon policing they are more likely to be enforcement oriented, looking for police to remove or shift rough-sleepers from public view.

Multi-agency work appears too limited and too informal at this stage to offer a meaningful alternative to enforcement policing, even though the shortcomings of enforcement as the main response to rough-sleeping are apparent to police and rough-sleepers alike. There is evidence of an expansion of multi-agency work in some areas. For example, within London there are moves to try to develop a multi-agency intervention project to tackle multiple alcohol, drug and mental health issues at the point of offending. A number of inter-agency training programmes are underway between street workers and police but they are still infrequent and the exception rather than commonplace. Similarly, police officers are becoming more involved in town centre and community safety partnerships which offer wider options for policing street homelessness.

Yet the pace of partnership development is slow and working alternatives to enforcement policing are few on the ground. Increasing multi-agency work on street homelessness is a priority if the 2002 Government targets for reducing rough-sleeping are to be met.

Officers' views of policing street homelessness

Police officers of all ranks see street homelessness as a matter beyond the scope of police to resolve and a prime example of the police as a 24-hour service picking up wider 'social' problems which are more appropriately handled by other agencies. Rough-sleeping is associated closely with alcohol misuse, increasingly overlapping with drug misuse and mental health related problems, all of which are difficult to police effectively. For most officers effective policing is a combination of incident management and law enforcement.

There is widespread concern across all ranks that police custody is not appropriate for people under the influence of alcohol or drugs or suffering from mental illness. Apprehension about 'death in custody', the demands which such prisoners place upon colleagues who have to watch over them whilst in custody, and the difficulties in getting a consistent, structured input from other agencies underpin officers' views of street homelessness.

Officers recognise the extent of victimisation experienced by rough-sleepers and are not indifferent to it. But they feel constrained by working on individual incidents which constantly highlight the policing difficulties in obtaining reliable evidence or ensuring the continued whereabouts of both victim and witnesses. Officers view their role in victim support taking place as part of the initial incident management followed by an onward referral to a more appropriate agency. The absence of accessible or appropriate victim support services for rough-sleepers is understood but it is not seen as a policing issue.

Offending by rough-sleepers is a persistent feature of policing areas where rough-sleepers live. Most offending is minor public order and, in officers' opinion, alcohol related. Rough-sleepers are often divided into two groups by officers. Small groups of longstanding rough-sleepers, often with alcohol problems, who come into police contact in three main ways – group drinking in public places when it is prohibited; internal squabbling within the group; and, minor offending which is mainly petty theft from off-licences and small shops or minor public order. Such groups are seen to be an enduring fact of policing, particularly in cities and towns, and are approached with a degree of resignation.

The second grouping is larger and more transient in that its membership shifts as people come on and off the streets. It may have a stable core of rough-sleepers known to police but it presents a broader range of policing problems. For many officers this grouping is increasingly associated with drug misuse overlapping into prostitution for women and a number of young men. From a police perspective, street homeless people in this group are more likely to be engaged in begging, sometimes aggressive begging; public order offences; street crime; and a larger proportion of thefts, primarily to support their addiction. Such groups are seen to be a more recent addition to policing and a source of concern because of their perceived potential for offending.

Enforcement is viewed by most officers as the basic tool in their police kit, sometimes the only workable tool. Liaison with other services is largely informal. There is some networking but persevering with it depends upon a willing response from other services. Many officers find alternatives to formally processing rough-sleepers, particularly those with alcohol problems. At a local level individual officers become familiar with hostel and other support services which will 'accept' rough-sleepers who might otherwise be formally processed. However, most are of the view that there are too few such facilities and that more formal liaison might help provide a consistent alternative to formal processing. Knowledge of local facilities and the development of a working network are seen to be products of their own initiative and not products from training or official force strategy.

Police officers have few illusions about the shortcomings of formally processing rough-sleepers but they believe they have no working alternative to straightforward enforcement. Current processes are seen to be neither deterrent nor cure. The potential for reducing street homelessness is seen to rest more with other agencies than police which, in part, reflects officers' view that they are the social service of last resort.

Overall, rough-sleeping is not seen as a policing priority even amongst those officers who are in daily contact with street homelessness. It is a recurring demand which must be policed but it is not to the forefront of officers' perspectives on local policing which are more likely to be focused upon what is seen to be more serious offending such as burglary, autocrime and crimes of violence. This may be due in part to a low policing value being associated with policing rough-sleepers – a low policing value is often associated with issues which provide little visible return for officers. It may also reflect a policing reality – police officers respond to a raft of demands on every shift. Unless a particular problem or a particular section of the community reaches a repeat offending level which demands wider action it is more likely that incidents will be policed individually. A by-product of pushing the policing of street homelessness out to individual officers, which occurs in all but those places with highest numbers of rough-sleepers, may be to individualise the policing response for police officer and rough-sleeper alike.

'Zero tolerance' policing and street homelessness

'Zero tolerance' policing has acquired some public prominence in the UK over the past two years. It has become associated in some sections of the community with high profile policing, particularly the policing of public areas. The debate has raised expectations that a new policing style might deliver answers to longstanding problems. It has also raised concern in some quarters that socially excluded sections of the community, including people who sleep rough, would be on the receiving end of any shift in police working. As is often the case there is a disparity between rhetoric and reality. It might be useful for the ongoing debate on 'zero tolerance' to consider briefly the relevant findings from this investigation into street homelessness and crime.

'Zero tolerance' has its origins in the thesis that minor violations of the law create a disorderly environment that encourages more crime (see Wilson and Kelling, 1982). Translated into policing terms any offence, however minor, should not go unchallenged and particular attention should be paid to offending in public which is seen to have the most detrimental effect if permitted to continue. Its application in New York in the early 1990s under the aegis of the Police Commissioner William Brattan is credited, in some quarters, with a reduction in the overall recorded crime figures of 37 per cent and the homicide rate of 50 per cent in three years. This has been taken as justifying its applicability to the UK. It is time to put it to rest for policing street homelessness.

The zero tolerance policing debate continues and has not been assisted by two factors – a growing willingness to apply the term 'zero tolerance' to describe any public policy which people wish to present as non-negotiable and an over-simplistic presentation that 'zero tolerance' policing involves nothing other than hard-handed enforcement policing and the maintenance of public order. Against this backcloth it is perhaps worth putting 'zero tolerance' policing in New York into wider context.

Public order policing was only one of a number of components enlisted in what was a two-pronged strategy to re-engineer the New York Police Department and create a more coherent and effective police service for the city. It is, unfortunately, the component which was taken up by the media as the most newsworthy and the aspect which is now most associated in the public mind with 'zero tolerance' policing. Over a two-year period New York police developed eight crime control strategies to address drugs, guns, youth crime, auto theft, corruption, traffic, domestic violence and quality of life crime. Crimes committed by rough-sleepers, including the infamous 'squeegee' crime, form a subset of the quality of life strategy. William Brattan reports that all eight components were subject to local community consultation, before, during and after their initial preparation (Brattan, 1998).

At the same time two major structural changes were introduced – an additional 7,000 police officers were recruited and deployed and a raft of management accountability and performance measures were put into place for local commanders. The former added substantial live resources to the police department whilst the latter rendered senior and middle management more accountable for tackling crime in their area.

The jury is still out on the overall success of 'zero tolerance' policing. It is undeniable that crime figures in New York have fallen and that public opinion surveys confirm that New Yorkers have a renewed belief in their safety. However, it is also the case that crime figures have fallen equally, if not more, in other US cities such as San Diego which have not pursued what is known as 'zero tolerance' policing. Recorded crime figures are falling year on year across most industrial nations, including Britain. Falling crime levels in New York may owe more to a larger, more efficient police department than any particular sub-operation focused on rough-sleepers.

The crimes reduced by the greatest margin in New York are largely major crimes including murder, rape, robbery and assault. These are not crimes usually associated with rough-sleepers. Crimes committed by rough-sleepers are usually less serious. This is a clear finding from this investigation. Offences committed by street homeless people in the UK are most often minor offences arising from their public lifestyle. They occur in the public eye, which raises their profile but they are not by and large predatory upon the public.

More importantly the findings show that enforcement policing, as suggested by the revised version of 'zero tolerance', is unable to successfully address street homelessness and crime. A narrow enforcement approach is more likely to increase the formal processing of rough-sleepers for minor offences and extend rather than reduce their social exclusion. It locks both police and rough-sleepers into an already unproductive cycle. It also lessens the likelihood of developing the wider partnership options, which are needed to reduce victimisation and offending amongst people who sleep rough.

But this is to analyse what, for the UK, is largely a straw man. There is no evidence across UK police forces of any support in policy or strategy for a 'zero tolerance' approach to policing rough-sleeping. In fact, the opposite is most often the case. Where street homelessness is seen to be a policing issue, both police force and officers across ranks, view it as an issue which cannot be resolved successfully by police alone.

It may be that an over-reliance upon enforcement policing arises from the tendency to push responsibility out to individual officers rather than adopt a force-wide strategy and from the absence of wider partnership options. It may also be that a concentration upon offending rather than a more balanced approach, which also tries to tackle victimisation, results in too much formal processing for no gain. However, these are not the outcomes of a planned 'zero tolerance' type approach to policing street homelessness in the UK. They are better seen as default outcomes which have arisen because we have not given adequate priority to working across agencies to address street homelessness. This does not make it any easier for rough-sleepers or police. The task is having recognised these shortcomings that appropriate action is taken to overcome them. However defined, 'zero tolerance' policing is not the answer.

Next steps

Policing people who sleep rough is a regular, frustrating and largely unrewarding experience for some police officers and almost all rough-sleepers. Relatively few officers, mainly street officers in a number of urban and metropolitan centres, police rough-sleeping as a daily feature of local policing. Most police officers have irregular contact with people who sleep rough. But most rough-sleepers have regular contact with police.

Where contact takes place it is mainly police initiated, arising from conflict between rough-sleepers' public lifestyles and the policing of public spaces. Officers have access to few policing options other than enforcement even in those areas where rough-sleeping is more commonplace. Local officers build informal networks with homelessness agencies, particularly outreach workers and hostels, but are continually pushed back upon enforcement as the only readily available tool in the policing toolkit. This takes place despite officers' longstanding recognition that enforcement on its own is not a solution and adds to officers' frustration.

Multi-agency work is increasing but it is underdeveloped and often focuses on responses to specific aspects of rough-sleeping such as begging or drinking in public places. This is understandable but it is not helpful. It reflects the way in which offending dominates how rough-sleeping is policed. But, more importantly, it makes it more likely that policing rough-sleeping will continue to be locked into the 'offending-enforcement-processing' cycle which helps neither rough-sleepers nor police.

Three areas are key if we are to successfully break away from offender driven policing for street homelessness to the mutual benefit of rough-sleepers and police, namely:

- uplifting multi-agency work on policing street homelessness (so police are involved more directly in the work of street homelessness co-ordinating groups and that working connections are made between street homelessness groups and community safety partnerships);
- widening policing options beyond enforcement (so officers are able to refer rough-sleepers throughout the 24-hour day; communicate easily with street outreach teams; and divert rough-sleepers away from formal processing);
- promoting consistency and good practice across police forces (so that the extent of victimisation amongst rough-sleepers is recognised and addressed; that officers have access to best practice to help them locally; and, that partnerships are boosted by experiences across UK forces).

5. Making improvements

Street homelessness and crime has a number of characteristics. Victimisation is hidden, high and personal. Offending is minor, repeated and public. Contact with police is regular, police initiated and derives mainly from offending. The outcome is formal, isolated and largely unproductive. Police and rough-sleepers alike are dissatisfied. Police officers see a low-level, but recurring social problem; it takes up police time and resources yet remains intractable and unsolved. Rough-sleepers see two street facts – a constant threat to personal safety which appears unnoticed and frequent contact with police officers which revolves them through the criminal justice system. The wider public sees vulnerable people, who come in and out of view, and who are most visible when their behaviour attracts attention.

The composite picture epitomises rough-sleepers' social exclusion. Rough-sleepers' exclusion from the social and economic mainstream catches them every way. It is the backcloth to above average contact with police. It raises their vulnerability to crime, particularly crimes against the person. It contributes to their offending, although it is not the sole reason. It revolves them without intervention through the criminal justice system. It pushes them to the visible margins and it helps keep them there.

Above all, exclusion inhibits solutions which cut across services. By lowering rough-sleepers' priority across all services except where rough-sleepers are themselves defined as being the problem, it makes it more likely that agencies will end up 'managing' rough-sleeping rather than 'solving' it because solutions require a sustained priority whilst management tends to focus upon daily demand.

There is room for improvement. In this section we set out the views of people who sleep rough on what they believe should be done to tackle victimisation, reduce offending and improve contact with police. We also explore the actions police officers believe are important for improving the policing of people who sleep rough.

These are the views of those who live and work on the street. They are not always comfortable or easily accommodated. They reflect fear, concern, frustration and a desire for rapid action. They are essentially practical views which address the immediacy of their situation but they are important benchmarks for rough-sleepers and police. They need to be incorporated into service design and any wider proposals on victim support, intervention, diversion, crime reduction and partnership if those proposals are to have currency amongst police officers and rough-sleepers. Listening to the wishes of rough-sleepers and police officers is a litmus test for the seriousness with which we are tackling social exclusion.

The final chapter brings together the structural and practical proposals which arise from the investigation.

Rough-sleepers on tackling victimisation and reducing offending

Most rough-sleepers believe safe housing to be the best way to disconnect street homelessness and crime. This is self-explanatory yet it highlights the importance of providing safer alternatives to the street if rough-sleepers are to be attracted away from street homelessness. The ways in which we provide housing pathways from street homelessness were beyond the scope of this investigation. However, despite the harshness and personal danger of rough-sleeping, hostels and other first steps away from the streets are often seen by rough-sleepers as more dangerous than sleeping rough. Although it was not a direct aspect of the investigation a number of rough-sleepers reported their unwillingness to use hostels and other centres because they were physically dangerous and theft of personal belongings was commonplace. Rosenblatt (1999) reports similar difficulties in New York where a number of longer-term rough-sleepers were attracted away from the streets only after action had been taken to substantially improve personal safety within hostels. It is an area which merits further investigation but there is adequate indirect evidence to suggest it needs to be a priority, particularly for reducing victimisation.

Safe housing aside, rough-sleepers' believe victimisation can be tackled in three ways:

- by directly addressing personal safety and theft from the person
- through changes in police patrolling
- by increasing the range and number of self-help organisations.

Fewer than one in 25 (four per cent) rough-sleepers believe that personal safety cannot be improved (see Table 5.1).

Just over one in three (35 per cent) people who sleep rough believe the most effective way of tackling high levels of victimisation would be to provide designated safe public areas, with or without a roof, where rough-sleepers could sleep, particularly at night. A further one in four (25 per cent) believe that having secure places to leave belongings would reduce repeated personal theft. Both views cut to the heart of the dangers of living on the street – personal safety and theft from the person, both of which are repeated experiences for the majority of rough-sleepers. It is understandable why these are high on the agenda yet it is harder to see how it might work.

Providing secure places for belongings seems the more straightforward so long as such places are also used as points of wider contact and intervention with rough-sleepers. Intervention would appear to be key. Safe sleeping places, however achieved, and secure places for belongings are legitimate and not unreasonable aspirations. But on their own they may have limited impact upon personal safety and without intervention there is a danger they might maintain continued rough-sleeping rather than creating a basis for leaving the streets.

This is not to argue that improving rough-sleepers' personal safety ought to take second place to leaving the streets or that we should not tackle victimisation for the false concern that safer streets might be more attractive to rough-sleepers. There is no evidence to suggest that high levels of victimisation act as an incentive to leaving the streets. Witness the existing hidden levels of victimisation endured by people who sleep rough and evidence suggests such experiences further exclude rough-sleepers and act as barriers to leaving the street because they further fragment an already unstable existence.

Any argument holding that people are more likely to leave the streets when life is too uncomfortable is mistaken. A few may do so but such a spur is likely to be successful only when the individual is already facing that direction and amenable to making a transition from the street. For the majority, additional hardship is just another survival issue which pushes them further into living from day-to-day and undermines the possibility of gaining any longer term control over their lives.

The provision of secure places for belongings could be linked to the provision of other services such as health, washing and laundry but conditional upon those services providing an opportunity for intervention. The need for secure places for belongings is proven. The potential benefit for rough-sleepers is high. The opportunity for constructive intervention should not be under-estimated.

Providing secure public areas for sleeping is harder to work through. Designating particular public areas may be a difficult public step to take for fear that it supports and maintains rough-sleeping. Yet, in many urban areas, this already exists unofficially. Rough-sleeping takes place and is sometimes 'tolerated' in a few run-down, non-residential, excluded areas where people who sleep rough have gathered, often for years. One advantage of piloting designated 'safe havens' could be the opportunity to deliver services en bloc and the possibility of cross-service intervention to help rough-sleepers leave the street. More importantly, it could be an opportunity to build victim support, offence reduction and criminal justice diversion programmes into the re-alignment of existing direct services in areas of highest need.

Despite understanding rough-sleepers' desire for places of safety, it is difficult not to see the designation of public areas for rough-sleeping as potential ghettos for street homelessness. Such areas are no substitute for safe, roofed alternatives which brings us back to the need to provide sufficient, adequate, accessible, safe places off the streets which can attract rough-sleepers. It re-emphasises the need to make hostels safe and to build personal safety into all aspects of first step accommodation away from the street.

A demand for safe places on the street arises from the wish to be safer in public and from a view that there are too few safe alternatives. The reality is that to reduce the victimisation of rough-sleepers we need to do both – make sure hostels and temporary accommodation are safer and make sure those areas where rough-sleepers congregate are as safe as possible.

Whatever the improvements are for directly addressing the victimisation experienced by rough-sleepers, there is also a need for further policing developments which rough-sleepers believe would reduce victimisation and make their lives safer. Just over one in five (22 per cent) people who sleep rough believe that policing changes would reduce victimisation. Three actions are sought:

- increased police patrols (which are seen as reassuring despite the frequency with which they lead to formal police contact)

- a greater police presence late at night when pubs and clubs are closing (a period when many rough-sleepers feel vulnerable to abuse and attack)
- greater informal contact between rough-sleepers and police (which is seen to provide a better understanding of rough-sleepers' experience as victims and help focus police attention).

Rough-sleepers in London are more likely than those in Swansea or Glasgow to see police as having a greater role to play in improving their safety. Just over one in three (35 per cent) rough-sleepers in London believe increased police patrols and greater contact would reduce victimisation. In contrast rough-sleepers in Glasgow see little role for police in improving their safety and are more insistent upon the need for safe areas to sleep (42 per cent) and secure places to leave belongings (42 per cent). These findings echo the dissatisfaction levels expressed by rough-sleepers about their contact with police and the extent to which safety is seen to be related to particular places.

Tackling offending

But, what of offending? What do street homeless people believe might reduce their offending? Fewer than one in 16 (6 per cent) rough-sleepers believe little can be done. Their solutions give greater emphasis to reducing the perceived need to offend than greater policing. (Please see figure 5.1)

One in three (34 per cent) people who sleep rough are of the view that regular access to food and support services reduces offending, particularly theft from shops. Just under one in three (28 per cent) believe that having safe public areas where rough-sleepers could gather at night or during the day would in itself reduce offending, particularly public order offending and incidents which arise through their public behaviour. It is an interesting proposition and it reflects a legitimate desire for places to go to where rough-sleepers are allowed to be. It is the case that being off the street attracts less police attention and reduces the likelihood of formal processing.

The Metropolitan Police Street Homelessness Unit analysis of the timing and spread of offending involving police in Charing Cross Division shows that police contact and arrests rise between 4pm and

Table 5.1 Rough-sleepers' views on tackling victimisation, reducing offending and improving contact with the police

On tackling victimisation		
Tackling safety directly:		
Designated public safe areas for sleeping	78	35%
Secure places to leave belongings	57	25%
Policing-related changes:		
Increased police patrols (particularly at closing time for pubs and clubs)	50	22%
Self-help:		
Improved organisation amongst rough-sleepers	31	14%
Not possible to reduce victimisation	9	4%
On reducing offending		
Changes to assist rough-sleepers:		
Regular access to support services and food	76	34%
Designated public safe areas for rough-sleepers	62	28%
Policing-related changes:		
Increased patrols/Greater contact	36	16%
Permitting drinking in public places	37	16%
Not possible to reduce offending	14	6%
On improving contact with the police		
Police-related changes:		
Specialised homelessness training	46	20%
Police homelessness unit	32	14%
More consistency in policing	32	14%
Greater informal contact	14	6%
Less formal contact	20	9%
Permitting drinking in public places	48	21%
Self-help		
More *Big Issue*-type initiatives	37	16%

** Percentage totals may be more or less than 100% due to rounding figures*

6pm for two reasons – most rough-sleepers are on the streets because it offers an opportunity to beg and seek support from commuters heading for home *and* because it coincides with the closure of day centres and is before the opening of night shelters.

The provision of safe places off the street during both day and night would appear to be key to reducing offending. It may be possible to reduce day-time offending by reducing the amount of time spent on the street by providing day centres and making sure their opening overlaps with night shelters and hostels. This should reduce the conflict between rough-sleepers' public lifestyle and the need for police to police public places. Likewise, just as safe overnight accommodation is key to reducing victimisation it is also likely to reduce offending.

Permitting drinking in specified public areas is seen by one in six (16 per cent) rough-sleepers as a constructive way of reducing offending. Given the overlap between street homelessness and problems with alcohol, the banning of drinking in public places brings many rough-sleepers into regular, formal contact with police. This may be the case even where the ban has been introduced to tackle wider issues of public drinking than several small groups of rough-sleepers. It is undoubtedly the case that bans upon drinking in public places fall heavily upon rough-sleepers and can increase offending rates. It is also the case that decriminalising drinking in public places would reduce offending by people who sleep rough.

This is a classic social exclusion conundrum. An action is invoked because it is seen to be in the public interest for most of the community – reducing drinking in public places may make those places safer for everyone. Yet, its impact upon a small, socially excluded section is much greater than it is upon those towards whom it was targeted. Rough-sleepers are no longer able to drink in public places without being arrested and processed through the criminal justice system. The others, against whom the ban was targeted, mainly young men are constrained from drinking in public but have access to alternatives, public houses and clubs.

Having alternatives is the key. The solution may not be to permit drinking in specified public places but to permit controlled drinking in places where rough-sleepers gather – day centres and wet hostels. This may pose difficulties in managing some premises but it reduces the conflict between drinking in public, rough-sleepers' public lifestyle and the need to police public spaces. The reduction in conflict may result in a reduction in offending. Wet facilities for rough-sleepers, however difficult to manage, may hold an important key to controlled drinking and reduced offending.

Interestingly, police action is seen by fewer rough-sleepers to have a role in reducing offending than it has in tackling victimisation. One in six (16 per cent) rough-sleepers believe that increased police patrolling at night and greater contact between rough-sleepers and police may reduce offending. Just over one in five (22 per cent) believe that similar police action may reduce victimisation. For some rough-sleepers police action is both deterrence and reassurance but it runs a distant second to actions which affect rough-sleepers' lifestyles in their view of how best to reduce offending.

Given the importance of contact between police and rough-sleepers for policing street homelessness, for reducing social exclusion and the level of processing through the criminal justice system, what do rough-sleepers' believe should be done to improve that contact?

Not surprisingly, two in three (63 per cent) rough-sleepers believe the key to improving contact with police lies in changes to the way police work. However, most of those changes look at ways in which police officers' view people who sleep rough. One in five (20 per cent) think police officers should receive specialised training in working with people who sleep rough and one in seven (14 per cent) believe police should set up a police homelessness unit to guide work with homeless people. Such changes are seen to underpin greater understanding of rough-sleepers' amongst police officers and lead to less formal processing.

When it comes to contact itself, rough-sleepers' would like to see it improved. They would like to see greater consistency, less formal contact and more informal contact. The most common request, from one in seven (14 per cent), is for more consistency in police contact. This may arise from specialised training but it reflects rough-sleepers' concerns that police contact can be unpredictable. It may, more often than not, lead to formal processing, but a number of people who sleep rough dislike the unpredictability of such contact. For them it is a reminder of their exclusion and they feel at the whim of some police officers' discretion. Rough-sleepers would like to see formal contact reduced and informal contact increased.

For some rough-sleepers, removing bans on drinking in public places or designating certain areas where public drinking is permitted would improve their lives as well as unilaterally improving contact with police. One in five (21 per cent) rough-sleepers believe police contact has increased and deteriorated since the introduction of public drinking bye-laws. Where such bye-laws exist there is an obligation upon police to enforce and to do so evenhandedly. In reality this has a disproportionate impact upon rough-sleepers.

Again, part of the solution may lie in access to wet facilities, particularly during daytime hours. We know that on-street drinking is attractive to some rough-sleepers. It is how they meet friends and acquaintances. Trying to ban such gatherings appears unproductive. It creates a merry-go-round as rough-sleepers continuously seek places, often out of the public eye, where they can drink for a few days before being discovered and moved on. It reduces the public visibility of street drinking. It does not remove it.

Rough-sleepers with long-term alcohol problems are amongst the more difficult groups to access and help leave the street. Having them involved in a continual merry-go-round works against intervention. Police officers and outreach workers are sometimes better served when they know where any rough-sleeper groups are likely to be. It can, paradoxically, be easier to police and less demanding upon time and resources. Given the apparent conflict between the general public's

Figure 5.1 Tackling victimisation, reducing offending and improving policing street homelessness

Rough-sleepers believe levels of victimisation and offending could be reduced by:

- providing safe places, with or without a roof, where rough-sleepers could sleep at night
- providing accessible, secure places to leave belongings
- regular access to food and support services, such as laundry and housing advice

Contact with the police could be improved by:

- providing training for police officers on street homelessness
- setting up more self-help initiatives similar to the *Big Issue*
- establishing a special police homelessness team or contact point whom they could trust

Police Officers seek three changes to help reduce victimisation and offending and to assist in the policing of street homelessness, namely:

- other agencies providing services for street homeless people across the 24 hour day to give officers wider options than arrest
- drug and alcohol detoxification facilities to divert rough-sleepers with drink and drug-related problems away from police cells and into more appropriate support services
- a means of contacting other services quickly and reliably so there is the possibility of intervention rather than circulating rough-sleepers through the system

wishes about drinking in public places and the lifestyle of some rough-sleepers it may be better to provide wet facilities where drinking can be managed and rough-sleepers can be contacted and policed rather than trying to enforce a widespread ban which is in many ways unenforceable, except through repeated processing.

Approximately one in six (16 per cent) people who sleep rough believe that more self-help initiatives, such as the *Big Issue*, would improve contact with police. For rough-sleepers these initiatives have a number of concurrent benefits. They provide access to income, albeit limited, and they provide some stability upon which they can build. But, perhaps more importantly in this context, they legitimise their presence on the streets and, in most instances, reduce the likelihood of formal contact with police. Even where relations are less good, Big Issue type initiatives give rough-sleepers legitimacy in their own eyes and are seen to be one way of managing relations with police.

Surprisingly few rough-sleepers believe that little can be done to tackle victimisation, reduce offending and improve relations with police. A considerable majority want to see changes. They have clear views of what needs to be done. Their proposals may not eliminate the problems but they are likely to go some considerable way to making their lives safer and helping a number of them to leave the street. For this alone, they are valuable and need to be pursued.

Police officers' priorities for policing street homelessness

Changes that help police officers to police street homelessness more easily and effectively dominate officers' priorities. They reflect the police view that working with rough-sleepers is a fact of life for some officers and, whilst repeated and low level, it is not a significant policing priority. Police officers seek three kinds of changes – those which provide more appropriate services at times when officers need them; those which provide specialist services alongside police so the needs of some rough-sleepers can be better addressed; and, improved communication with other agencies to speed up contact and increase the possibility of early intervention (see Figure 5.1).

Enforcement is not a policing priority, although it may be the most exercised option just now. Officers would rather get beyond enforcement which they see as essential in some circumstances but largely inappropriate for dealing with the range of low-level, nuisance offending undertaken by most rough-sleepers.

Police officers are acutely aware that their status as a 24-hour service brings them into contact with people who might be better served by other care and social service agencies, many of whom are unavailable at the point when they are most needed by police. From a police perspective, contact with people who sleep rough often comes into this category. It is better dealt with by others who are not available yet it cannot be left alone so it is managed by enforcement as the only available option.

Officers will try to develop informal methods of disposal wherever they are available. It is not uncommon for officers to guide or deliver rough-sleepers to hostels providing they are open, places are regularly available and there is a working relationship with police. The need for a working relationship should not be under-estimated. Police officers are unlikely to pursue relations with hostels or services if staff are unhelpful or unwilling to assist when they arrive. There is little value for them as people or as police officers if the limited services which may be available are inaccessible or sometimes unco-operative. In these circumstances it is easier and safer to formally process the rough-sleepers, however unproductive this might be.

A police priority is the availability of care and social services for rough-sleepers across the 24-hour day. In officers' view everyone would benefit. Police would have increased options and time and resources would be better applied on other policing matters. Police involvement would be restricted to onward referral or assisted referral unless the situation required formal policing. It would improve relations between rough-sleepers and police because less contact should lead to formal processing and police could be seen as providing initial assistance in more instances than they can just now. Rough-sleepers would receive appropriate assistance and be diverted at a minor level away from offending and formal police contact. Services would benefit from improved liaison with police.

But, this requires a number of actions to make it work. Adequate, safe facilities for rough-sleepers are a priority. Rough-sleepers are unlikely to be willing to go to unsafe places even if the alternative is formal processing by police. Police are unlikely to be willing to refer rough-sleepers to unsafe facilities. Co-ordination between services and agencies is necessary to make sure there is 24-hour coverage of appropriate services. We have already seen that gaps in service are likely to lead to increased police contact (see Chapter 4). Resources are needed to make it happen, either by redirecting existing resources or by pump-priming the changes with additional short-term finances. The benefits are likely to be substantial for rough-sleepers, police and welfare agencies.

Detoxification facilities

Building upon the need for basic 24-hour cover by services other than police, officers believe there is a growing need for specialised detoxification facilities, particularly in urban areas where there are a number of rough-sleepers. Police believe that police cells are not appropriate places for rough-sleepers with drug, alcohol or even mental health difficulties. Officers fear becoming involved in a death in custody and see this as an almost inevitable outcome of the increase in overlapping problems which some rough-sleepers suffer. Few such facilities exist across the UK. Where they do, such as in Aberdeen, police believe they are helpful alternatives which assist them in policing rough-sleeping as well as others with drink or drug-related difficulties.

The debate over detoxification facilities is long and well documented. The primary reason why so few facilities exist is cost. A cost-benefit analysis of the failure to provide a number of detoxification facilities is beyond the remit of this investigation. Yet, it is evident that there is a high cost for repeated use of police time and resources handling situations involving rough-sleepers, drugs and alcohol in some areas. There is a high human cost for rough-sleepers. Investment in detoxification facilities may be necessary to reduce recurring costs from managing drug and alcohol related problems at a later stage. This would benefit police, rough-sleepers and others with drug and alcohol problems.

Officers, particularly urban police officers, report an increase in drug misuse and an increasing overlap with other problems such as alcohol misuse. Detoxification facilities would provide an opportunity for early intervention and restructure the relationship between police and some rough-sleepers.

24-hour partnership

Improved communication between police and other agencies is seen by most police officers to be an essential development if there is to be a reduction in circulating rough-sleepers through the system. A number of areas, including Edinburgh and central London, have been piloting improved communication between police and street homelessness agencies. But, there is still some way to go to meet the aspirations of police officers who are looking for a simple method of contacting other agencies to provide information about new arrivals on the street or to connect with outreach workers and guide them towards non-offending rough-sleepers.

As a 24-hour service police are often the first agency to come into contact with rough-sleepers as they arrive on the street. Evidence suggests that the earlier the intervention the easier it may be to help someone leave the street (see SEU, 1998). There may be benefit in establishing a 24-hour contact point between police and outreach services whereby patrol officers are able to relay information to outreach workers quickly and reliably. This already exists informally in some areas but it does so as a working relationship between individual officers and outreach workers and not as a structured relationship between agencies. It is hard to sustain, particularly when staff move on or get transferred, and it rarely develops beyond individual casework. This limits its usefulness and potential. A more structured relationship is likely to be more productive and enduring and to lead to further working developments between police officers and outreach workers.

Police officers' priorities reflect the growth of partnership thinking across UK forces but they also indicate the amount of work which is yet to be done if we are to be able to shift away from an over-reliance upon enforcement in policing people who are street homeless. Working in partnership is key to making the changes police wish to see in widening the availability of care and social services; establishing specialist drug and alcohol detoxification facilities; and, providing reliable 24-hour communication between officers and outreach teams. It requires consistent police input to the appropriate partnership structures if it is to be realised.

Next steps

Rough-sleepers and police officers have an interest in tackling victimisation, reducing offending and improving contact between themselves. For rough-sleepers it is key to a safer, less dangerous life, where offending is less of a daily occupation required to survive and where police contact is less formal and less likely to lead to processing through the criminal justice system. For police officers it offers reduced demand upon time and resources, less time spent formally processing rough-sleepers for little benefit and access to a range of services which assist officers in delivering the kind of police service they prefer to deliver. For both it means reduced frustration and the likelihood of less conflict.

Not all the proposals are easily implemented. But many are demonstrably commonsense and reflect the legitimate aspirations of rough-sleepers and police alike. A number of tasks have to be undertaken if we are to meet these wishes and aspirations, including:

- improving rough-sleepers' personal safety both on and off the street (which means looking at secure places for personal belongings and revisiting police patrolling as well as designating 'safe havens' and reviewing safety in hostels and temporary accommodation)
- reducing formal contact and increasing informal contact between rough-sleepers and police (which means ensuring overlapping services throughout the day to reduce rough-sleepers' time in the public and police eye; tackling drinking in public places by providing wet facilities; reviewing existing policing practices, including liaison; and, extending joint work and training between police and street homelessness agencies)
- widening options for both police and rough-sleepers (which means providing appropriate care and social services, particularly detoxification facilities, at times when officers and rough-sleepers need access; setting up 24-hour contact between police and other agencies; and, supporting self-help initiatives for rough-sleepers which amongst other benefits can improve safety and reduce offending)

Few rough-sleepers or police officers believe that nothing can be done to reduce victimisation and offending or to improve contact between people who sleep rough and police. But many believe there is little will to implement the changes they wish to see.

6. Conclusion and recommendations

From almost every angle the present situation is less than satisfactory. Street homelessness and crime appear locked in a self-sustaining loop which only impinges upon the wider community through its public visibility as begging or drinking in public. Otherwise it goes largely unnoticed except within the fairly closed world of rough-sleepers, police and street homeless organisations. Within the confines of the street homeless world, crime is seen as an intractable reality – a product of the conjunction between social exclusion and life on the street.

Rough-sleepers are hidden victims of crime with a frequency which would not be tolerated amongst the wider population. Victim support services are not a central feature of the homelessness landscape. Victimisation is at the same time a benchmark and a consequence of rough-sleepers' social exclusion. Frequent personal victimisation helps maintain and extend the social exclusion which goes hand in hand with street homelessness.

At the same time rough-sleepers' offending may be minor but it arises directly from their public lives and it gives rise to regular, formal contact with police. It places recurring demands upon police time and resources, particularly in urban areas, yet, with few exceptions it is a low policing priority which is delegated to community and beat officers to manage as and when demand occurs.

Police contact is largely driven by offending and pitches rough-sleepers into a mutually non-productive cycle processing them through the criminal justice system without intervention. This, in turn, reinforces rough-sleepers' exclusion making it more difficult to leave the street. Police officers have long recognised the futility of constantly processing rough-sleepers but they are not equipped to deliver the care and social service solutions essential to breaking the cycle. Enforcement remains the basic tool available to police officers to help manage and contain offending by rough-sleepers.

Multi-agency work may be increasing but it remains underdeveloped and limited. It is patchy and inconsistent, often dependent upon informal networking rather than planned liaison and pushed out by police and homelessness agencies to front-line police officers and outreach workers. As a result many multi-agency solutions are currently confined to individual incidents and casework, which is helpful to some rough-sleepers, but is hard to sustain or build into widespread good practice and is often lost with normal staff turnover.

Yet, there is cause for tempered optimism. The Rough-Sleepers' Initiative, despite its shortcomings, has highlighted the need for continuing improvements in inter-agency co-ordination and has started to provide better facilities and services. Extending the lead responsibility of the Department of the Environment, Transport and the Regions and setting up the joint Ministerial Committee to co-ordinate work on rough-sleeping are steps in the right direction. But there is some distance yet to travel. Too few police forces are active strategic players in multi-agency programmes. The absence of 24-hour street homelessness services beyond police greatly constrains policing options. Containment and enforcement rather than diversion and resolution still dominate the policing of street homelessness and crime.

At the same time Government plans on social exclusion and the recent Crime and Disorder Act (1998) offer potential impetus for local planning and service delivery through street homeless co-ordinators and for partnerships by linking street homeless work into local community safety strategies. Improved partnership working is an essential component for disconnecting street homelessness and crime. But unless it works to widen policing options, to generate diversion and intervention for rough-sleepers, and is supported by services which assist police work it could be a double-edged sword.

It is not difficult to envisage local community safety partnerships, from which rough-sleepers are excluded by nature of the partnership and their lifestyle, whose perspective on street homelessness stems from the public visibility of begging and drinking in public places and whose response is greater police enforcement. It is understandable but the opposite of what needs to be done. Without a shift within police forces towards partnership problem-solving on rough-sleeping and connections being made for community safety partnerships, local officers may come under added pressure to tackle street homelessness by enforcement – and this does not work. It is a short-term response to a longstanding problem which runs the risk of being tough on crime at the expense of being tough on the causes of crime.

This is not to say the crime and disorder legislation is flawed or that the Government's framework for tackling social exclusion is not working. Both are essentially sound steps. But, their outcome is, as yet, uncertain and their potential, as yet, unrealised. Policy and practice on social exclusion, street homelessness and crime have yet to be adequately brought together. This makes it timely for guidance and hopefully open for recommendations.

The issues seem straightforward – how do we tackle rough-sleepers' victimisation; reduce offending; break free from the revolving door of street homelessness-offending-processing; and shift the basis for policing away from unproductive enforcement onto problem-solving, thereby paving the way for reducing social exclusion? How do we do it in such a way as to overcome the disjunction between tackling social exclusion and crime and disorder? The investigation suggests a number of actions.

Reducing victimisation

Rough-sleepers' victimisation is high, repeated, personal and often violent. It is hidden from public view, excluded from official investigations of victimisation and crime, and seen as an intractable outcome of street homelessness. Reporting levels are akin to those found previously amongst other excluded victims. They are similar to earlier under-reporting of violence against women and racial harassment. Four areas need to be addressed by agencies, the emerging local street homelessness co-ordinating groups and local community safety partnerships:

- improving safety
- reducing personal victimisation and providing support to victims
- increasing reporting
- improving connections between street homelessness and community safety services

To improve rough-sleepers' safety, we need to:

- ensure places for first steps from the streets, particularly hostels, are themselves safer than the streets;
- develop specific multi-agency crime reduction packages for inner-city private rented accommodation areas which are the receivers of rough-sleepers as they leave the street;

- consider establishing pilot safe havens in urban areas where rough-sleepers' congregate within which to develop good local multi-agency packages for protecting rough-sleepers and reducing victimisation;
- review police patrolling, particularly at key times such as closing time for pubs and clubs in areas where rough-sleepers congregate, and increase informal contact between rough-sleepers and police to reassure people who sleep rough and at the same time reduce victimisation;

Recommendation 1

The Department for the Environment, Transport and the Regions (DETR) and the Home Office should set up a multi-agency short-life task group to review safety in hostels and temporary accommodation and bring forward recommended standards and good practice for improving personal safety for rough-sleepers in such accommodation.

Recommendation 2

Local street homelessness co-ordinating groups or in their absence local community safety partnerships should set up a joint review of safety in local hostels and temporary accommodation involving police, local authority housing and social services, and street homelessness agencies.

Recommendation 3

DETR and the Home Office in partnership with police forces and local street homelessness co-ordinating groups should establish a pilot Safe Havens programme in a small number of urban areas to develop best practice multi-agency packages for protecting rough-sleepers and reducing victimisation

Recommendation 4

All police forces should include an assessment of police patrolling patterns in areas where rough-sleepers congregate and bring forward proposals to increase informal contact between officers and people who are street homeless within a wider review of the policing of street homelessness across the force area.

To reduce personal victimisation of rough-sleepers and provide support to victims, we need to:

- establish inter-agency victim support outreach services to work alongside existing agencies and services but under the guidance and direction of the local inter-agency co-ordinating group – such a service to have three responsibilities:
  - to advise existing services in re-directing service delivery to include good practice on victim support;
  - to co-ordinate agencies and services' activities in tackling victimisation in the local area;
  - to develop and deliver appropriate victim support services for rough-sleepers;
- make a reduction in crimes of violence against rough-sleepers a priority for local multi-agency partnerships and set up specific repeat victim packages to help street homeless people (both to target specific offences and to provide victim support, which is currently not available to rough-sleepers)
- provide secure places for rough-sleepers to leave belongings to reduce victimisation, particularly personal theft (doing so alongside other services such as health, washing and laundry and accompanying the facility with increased contact and intervention).

Recommendation 5

Local street homelessness co-ordinating groups or in their absence local community safety partnership groups should come together with local victim support to:

- establish local inter-agency victim support services for street homeless people;
- prioritise a reduction in crimes of violence against rough-sleepers;
- set up repeat victimisation packages to tackle prevalent victimisation of rough-sleepers in the local area.

Recommendation 6

Street homeless service providers should review the needs of people who sleep rough in their area and consider how best to provide secure places alongside existing service provision for rough-sleepers to leave personal belongings.

To increase rough-sleepers' reporting of victimisation, we need to:

- introduce ways of building rough-sleepers' confidence in agencies, similar to those undertaken with victims of racial harassment and domestic violence, including, for example:
  - recording victim incidents by key agencies, including police and other front-line service deliverers
  - providing victim support services at key points of contact (including police stations, day centres and through outreach teams)

Recommendation 7

Street homelessness co-ordinating groups should include, as part of the local strategy for reducing rough-sleeping, a victimisation reporting programme which requires local front-line agencies to record victim incidents involving rough-sleepers and provides a published network of contact points for accessing victim support services.

To improve connections between street homelessness and community safety services so they do not cut across each other and further exclude rough-sleepers, we need to:

- ensure there is a working connection between local street homelessness co-ordinating groups and the local community safety partnerships emerging under the Crime and Disorder Act (1998)
- require local community safety partnerships to include rough-sleepers amongst the designated 'hard-to-reach' groups to be contacted and have their safety needs included in the local community safety strategy

Recommendation 8

DETR and the Home Office should issue joint guidance to police forces, local authorities and voluntary agencies on reducing victimisation, improving services to meet the needs of rough-sleepers as victims and inter-agency working between local community safety partnerships and street homelessness co-ordinating groups.

Recommendation 9

The Home Office should amend its guidance to local community safety partnerships under the Crime and Disorder Act (1998) to designate rough-sleepers as a 'hard-to-reach' group which must be consulted on its community safety needs and have provision made for it within the local strategy.

Reducing offending

Rough-sleepers' offending is high, repeated and largely minor. It arises from their public lifestyle and need. It is not a predatory threat to community safety. It brings rough-sleepers into regular police contact, takes up police time and resources and gives rise to regular formal processing through the criminal justice system without intervention. Three areas need to be addressed: reducing offending by rough-sleepers; reducing the proportion of rough-sleepers being formally processed for repeat minor offences; and, releasing police resources to concentrate upon more serious offending outwith people who are street homeless. The key to reducing offending and the key to helping rough-sleepers to leave the streets is structured intervention at those points where it is most likely to be heeded, be needed and to have an impact. Offending, however minor, is an opportunity for structured intervention and diversion which is currently being missed.

Four areas need to be addressed:

- Structured intervention and diversion from offending
- Providing facilities and support programmes for diversion
- Targeting repeat offending
- Reviewing and re-applying resources

To establish structured intervention and divert rough-sleepers from offending, we need to:

- set up structured intervention and diversion programmes for rough-sleepers at the point of offending (including multi-agency diversion and support programmes involving courts, police, voluntary agencies and probation)
- ensure diversion and offence reduction programmes are linked into the work of local street homelessness co-ordinating groups and community safety partnerships

Recommendation 10

The Home Office should take the lead, with the support of the Lord Chancellor's Department and DETR, in developing a pilot rough-sleepers' diversion programme which brings together multi-agency services along similar lines to those being applied for Youth Offender Teams

To provide facilities and support programmes for diverting rough-sleepers, we need to:

- introduce steps which reduce the likelihood of formal contact between police and rough-sleepers which are also likely to reduce offending, including:
    - day centres which provide places off the street
    - overlapping services throughout the day which help rough-sleepers reduce their time in the public and police eye
    - tackle drinking in public places by providing wet facilities, particularly during daytime but also at night, where rough-sleepers who want to drink can do so but in managed surroundings which also offer the opportunity for intervention;
- provide support services and regular access to food thereby, in the view of rough-sleepers, reducing the need for offending, particularly theft from shops;
- give priority to establishing alcohol and drug detoxification facilities in those areas with the greatest number of rough-sleepers and include support programmes for alcohol and drug misuse within street homelessness diversion projects;
- extend support for existing self-help initiatives and build other such programmes to help rough-sleepers support themselves and to legitimise relations with police at a time when formal processing may be unhelpful in helping some rough-sleepers leave the streets.

Recommendation 11

Street homeless co-ordinating groups should initiate a joint service review involving police and local service providers which brings forward ways of reducing formal contact between rough-sleepers and police and which looks, in particular, at the provision of day centres; the provision of 24-hour service cover; and, the provision of wet day and night facilities for rough-sleepers.

Recommendation 12

The Department of Health should work in partnership with the Home Office and local street homelessness co-ordinating groups to put in place drug and alcohol detoxification facilities and support programmes as part of a pilot rough-sleepers' diversion from custody programme.

Recommendation 13

Local street homelessness co-ordinating groups, existing service providers and the Department for Employment should review the present extent of self-help provision for rough-sleepers within the local area and bring forward proposals for wideining the application of New Deal for Employment opportunities for rough-sleepers.

To target offending by rough-sleepers and reduce it, we need to:

- target the most frequent types of minor offending and repeat offending for diversion (this should reduce the volume of offending)
- target the smaller number of more serious offences for prosecution such as serious assault, robbery and burglary committed by a smaller grouping within rough-sleepers (this should reduce serious offending and may well improve safety amongst rough-sleepers as well)
- target actions, such as theft from shops by providing regular access to food and clothing, which reduce the need for rough-sleepers' offending which, in the view of rough-sleepers, is more likely to reduce that offending than increased police action

Recommendation 14

Local street homelessness co-ordinating groups should work jointly with local community safety partnerships to prepare and include offence reduction plans within local rough-sleeping and community safety strategies.

To find the resources to meet the cost of diverting rough-sleepers from offending, we need to:

- provide seedcorn funding for diversion and support packages but meet ongoing revenue costs from potential savings to all services, including the criminal justice system

Recommendation 15
The Treasury, in partnership with the Home Office, should review current public expenditure arising from street homelessness and crime and bring forward proposals to meet the on-going costs of a diversion from custody programme by re-applying existing resources.

Policing people who sleep rough

Policing people who sleep rough is a regular, recurring demand upon police time and resources but it is not a UK policing priority nor is it a priority even within those urban forces for whom street homelessness is a feature of local policing. With few exceptions policing street homelessness is enforcement driven and delegated to local officers to police as and when required. Police officers are being asked to police street homelessness without recourse to care and social service provision which the police and the criminal justice system are not equipped to provide and are better delivered by other agencies. Three main areas need to be addressed if we are to successfully break away from offender driven policing for street homelessness to the mutual benefit of rough-sleepers and police alike:

- increasing police participation in street homelessness partnerships
- widening policing options beyond enforcement
- promoting consistency and good practice across police forces

To increase police participation in partnership, we need to:

- formally require police forces to become partners in local multi-agency strategic responses on street homelessness;
- require local street homeless co-ordinators to consult and involve senior police management in the preparation and delivery of street homelessness strategies;

- require local street homelessness strategies and programmes to include multi-agency proposals for policing street homelessness;
- require local street homeless co-ordinators to liaise with and be represented on local community safety partnership groups.

Recommendation 16

DETR and the Home Office should include in their guidance to police forces, local authorities, street homeless co-ordination groups, community safety partnerships and voluntary organisations the requirements for senior police involvement in strategic planning on street homelessness and local connections between community safety and street homelessness strategies.

To widen policing options beyond enforcement, we need to:

- encourage the development of one-stop, 24-hour contact projects for rough-sleepers to provide police officers with onward referral points for rough-sleepers who may need assistance but who have not committed any offences (this may also facilitate earlier identification of and intervention with people arriving on the street);
- provide appropriate local care and social services at times when police officers require access to them to reduce formal processing (overcome local gaps in service);
- provide specialist drug and alcohol detoxification services alongside police so the needs of some rough-sleepers can be better addressed.

Recommendation 17

Local street homelessness co-ordinating groups should work with local police forces to give priority to improving communication between front-line police officers and outreach teams and to providing one-stop, 24-hour contact points between the services.

To promote consistency and good practice across police forces, we need to encourage the development of consistent policing practices across the UK by issuing guidance in the following areas:

- appoint a street homelessness liaison officer at an appropriate rank within each police force and, if appropriate, set up a small liaison unit to boost multi-agency work, improve victim support and establish force training on street homelessness

- officer training (including good practice on policing street homelessness in probationer training, personal skills training and in-house force training)
- invite the National Police Training College and the Crime Prevention College to develop a short course and supporting good practice information for force street homelessness liaison officers (potentially drawing upon the emerging work of the Metropolitan Police Street Homelessness Unit)
- establish a pilot programme for recording victimisation of and offending by rough-sleepers for police forces with identified concentrations of street homeless people
- encourage senior police management and local street homeless co-ordinators to facilitate inter-agency training programmes involving police as trainers and trainees

Recommendation 18

All UK police forces should review the policing of street homelessness within the force area and, in particular, their arrangements for strategic partnership on street homelessness; their arrangements for co-ordinating and managing force policy and practice on street homelessness; changes to recording practices on crimes against rough-sleepers; and, the need for officer training.

Recommendation 19

Police and local street homelessness co-ordinating groups, or in their absence, local street homelessness service providers should arrange inter-agency staff training programmes for police officers and outreach staff.

Recommendation 20

The Home Office in partnership with the Association of Chief Police Officers and Police National Training organisations should develop and issue good practice guidance on policing street homelessness

Connecting social exclusion, street homelessness and crime

Recommendation 21

The Ministerial Committee on Rough-Sleeping, which has responsibility for overseeing the development and delivery of co-ordinated action on rough-sleeping, should review the findings and recommendations from this investigation and bring forward proposals to incorporate them into the Government's action plan for reducing rough-sleeping.

Injustice and inequity go hand in hand with social exclusion. Reducing social exclusion and helping rough-sleepers leave the street requires working connections between social exclusion and crime and disorder policies. Otherwise, we will perpetuate the policy shortcomings of the past 30 years which have repeatedly set initiatives to reduce rough-sleeping on a collision course with measures to tackle crime and disorder which have been increasingly directed towards managing public order. To make the connections we need to improve partnership working between police and street homeless agencies; tackle victimisation of rough-sleepers; develop and implement joint programmes to divert offending rough-sleepers away from the revolving doors of the criminal justice system; widen policing options beyond enforcement onto problem-solving policing; and, set up inter and intra-agency training programmes to establish good practice, support the shifts in policy and operations and transfer best practice. Need and good intent are widespread. But they have to be supported.

The author acknowledges that responsibility for carrying forward some of the recommendations in Scotland and Wales rests with the Scottish and Welsh executives and agencies within those countries and asks that they are pursued by the appropriate responsible authority.

Select bibliography

Anderson L and Snow DA (1993) *Down on Their Luck: A Study of Homeless Street People* Berkeley University of California Press

Aulette J and Aulette A (1987) *Police Harassment of the Homeless: The Political Purpose of the Criminalisation of Homelessness* Humanity and Society 11, 244-256

Barak G (1991) *Gimme Shelter: A Social History of Homelessness in Contemporary America* Praeger: New York

Barak G and Bohm RM (1989) *The Crimes of the Homeless or the Crime of Homelessness? On The Dialectics Of Criminalisation, Decriminalisation, And Victimisation* Contemporary Crises vol13, (pp275-288)

Baron S and Hartnagel T (1997) 'Attributions, Affect, and Crime: Street Youths' Reactions to Unemployment' *Criminology* vol 35, no 3, August (pp409-434)

Buss TF and Redburn FS (1986) *Responding to America's Homeless: Public Policy Alternatives* Praeger: New York

Carlen P (1996) *Jigsaw – A Political Criminology of Youth Homelessness* Buckingham: Open University Press

Chambliss, W (1964) *A Sociological Analysis of the Law of Vagrancy* Social Problems 12, 67-77

Council of Europe (1985) *Research on Victimisation* Collected Studies in Criminological Research, vol xxii (European Committee on Crime Problems: Strasbourg)

Crisis (1998a) *Begging and People Who Beg* (Crisis Fact Sheet: 28/03/98: London)

Crisis (1998b) *Bricks Without Mortar – 30 Years of Single Homelessness* London

Crisis (1994) *We are Human Too – A study of People Who Beg* London

Dennis N (1998) [ed] *Zero Tolerance: Policing a Free Society* Institute of Economic Affairs: London second ed

Department of the Environment (1996a) *Rough Sleepers Initiative: The Next Challenge* HMSO: London March

Department of the Environment (1996b) *From Street To Home: An Evaluation of Phase 2 of the Rough Sleepers Initiative* HMSO: London

Department of the Environment (1995) *Rough Sleepers Initiative: Future Plans* Consultation Paper linked to the Housing White Paper 'Our Future Homes' HMSO: London, October

Department of the Environment (1993) *The Rough Sleepers Initiative: An Evaluation* HMSO: London

Grenier P (1996) *Still Dying for a Home* Crisis: London

Greve J (1991) *Homelessness in Britain* Joseph Rowntree Foundation, September

Fattah EA (1994) *The Interchangeable Roles of Victim and Victimiser* Heuni Papers No 3 European institute for Crime Prevention and Control: Helsinki

Fischer PJ (1992a) 'Criminal Behaviour and Victimisation among Homeless People' in Jahiel, RI *Homelessness – A Prevention-orientated Approach* Baltimore: John Hopkins University Press

Fischer PJ (1992b) 'The Criminalization of Homelessness' in Greenblatt M & Robertson M [Eds] *Homelessness, A National Perspective* Plenum Press: New York

Foord M, Palmer J and Simpson D (1998) *Bricks Without Mortar – 30 Years of Single Homelessness* Crisis: London

Goldstein H (1990) *Problem-Oriented Policing* McGraw-Hill, New York

Home Office Research and Statistics Directorate (1996) *The 1996 International Crime Victimisation Survey* Research Findings No 57 Home Office: London

Home Office (1996) *The 1996 British Crime Survey* (Home Office Statistical Bulletin Issue 19/96: London: September

Home Office (1998a) *The 1998 British Crime Survey* (England and Wales) Home Office Statistical Bulletin 21/98: London, September

Home Office (1998b) *Concern About Crime: Findings from the 1998 British Crime Survey* (Home Office Research Findings 93, London

Hough M and Roberts J (1998) 'Attitudes to Punishment: Findings from the British Crime Survey', *Home Office Research Study 179* Home Office, London

Kress JB (1994) 'Homeless Fatigue Syndrome: The Backlash Against the Crime of Homelessness in the 1990s' *Social Justice* vol 21, 3 (pp85-108)

McCartney B and Hagan J (1991) 'Homelessness: A Criminogenic Situation' *British Journal of Criminology* 31, no4, Autumn (pp393-410)

Marshall T and Fairhead S (1979) 'How to keep homeless offenders out of prison' *New Society* 20/9/79 (pp616-617)

Moore J, Canter D, Stockley D & Drake M (1995) *The Faces of Homelessness in London* Dartmouth: Aldershot

NACRO (1998) *Going Straight Home – A Paper on Homelessness and Offenders* NACRO: London, February

O'Leary J (1997) *Beyond Help? Improving Service Provision for street homeless people with mental health and alcohol or drug dependency problems* National Homeless Alliance: London: August

Ramsay M (1996) *Housing for the Homeless Ex-Offender* Home Office Research Bulletin No20: London

Randall G and Brown S (1993) *The Rough Sleepers Initiative: An Evaluation* HMSO

Rosenblatt M formerly Assistant Director of Homeless Services, New York City, Personal Communication, (1999)

Snow DA, Baker SG and Anderson L (1989) 'Criminality and Homeless Men: An Empirical Assessment' *Social Problems* 36, no5, December (pp532-549)

Social Exclusion Unit (1998) *Bringing Britain Together: A National Strategy for Neighbourhood Renewal* Social Exclusion Unit, HMSO, London

Wilson JQ and Kelling GL (1982) 'Broken Windows' *Atlantic Monthly* pp29-38, March

Appendix I: technical information

Introduction

The independent investigation was funded by Crisis, the leading national homelessness charity, as part of its research on homelessness. It explored three aspects of rough-sleeping and crime:

- people who sleep rough as victims of crime
  - how often are rough-sleepers' victims?
  - what kinds of crime do they experience?
  - how does this experience (level and type of crime) compare to that of the general population?
  - are offences reported?
  - how fearful, if at all, are rough-sleepers of being victims of crime?
- crimes committed by people who sleep rough
  - what kinds of crime are committed by people who sleep rough?
  - are they arrested?
  - are they charged?
  - how do these crimes compare (in type and level) to those of which they are victims?
- policing street homelessness: contact between people who sleep rough and the police
  - how often do rough-sleepers and police come into contact?
  - what kinds of contact take place?
  - how satisfied or dissatisfied are rough-sleepers with police contact?
  - what actions would rough-sleepers like to see taken to tackle victimisation, reduce offending and improve contact with police?
- policing policies and practices
  - have forces adopted any particular policing policies, strategies or initiatives for policing street homelessness?
  - which policing style, if any, do police forces consider most appropriate and effective for policing people who sleep rough?

- what approaches are employed by police forces towards rough-sleepers as potential victims or offenders?
- what training or guidance, if any, is given to officers who are likely yo come into contact with rough-sleepers?
- are there any external influences upon your approach to street homelessness?
- what multi-agency or partnership initiatives are underway on street homelessness?
- what changes, if any, would police forces like to see in the policing of street homelessness?

Methodology

Fieldwork for the investigation into Street Homelessness and Crime took place between May 1998 and December 1998 on three sites – Glasgow, Swansea and London. The three sites were selected to provide coverage across Scotland, England and Wales: to enable comparison between rough-sleepers' experiences: and to reflect a potential range of policing styles. Strathclyde Police are pursuing high profile public policing through the 'Spotlight Initiative'. South Wales Police are pursuing community-based policing within Swansea City Centre. The Metropolitan Police have developed a range of policing reponses, including establishing a specialised street homelessness unit within Charing Cross Division. Four Police Divisions took part in the investigation: Glasgow City Centre Division (Strathclyde Police): Swansea South Division (South Wales Police): Charing Cross Division (Metropolitan Police) and Vauxhall Division (Metropolitan Police). All four Divisions are central city police divisions with a concentration of rough-sleepers.

The investigation included:

- Rough-sleepers:
  - six structured group discussions, two in each location, involving 42 people who were currently sleeping rough;
  - 120 in-depth, one-to-one, structured interviews with rough-sleepers (29 in Glasgow, 61 in London and 30 in Swansea) (demographic details are set out in figure A.1).

Figure A.1 Street homelessness and crime: rough-sleeper interviews

Men	99	83%
Women	21	18%
London	61	51%
Swansea	30	25%
Glasgow	29	24%
16 to 20 years	24	20%
21 to 29 years	49	41%
30 to 39 years	22	18%
40 to 49 years	14	12%
50 years and over	11	9%
UK White	96	80%
Irish	14	12%
Caribbean	3	3%
African	2	2%
Asian	1	1%
Other	3	3%

Interviews conducted between June 1998 and September 1998.

The fieldwork interviews were analysed using SPSS. Further details from scottballintyne@compuserve.com

The interviews were conducted by experienced street outreach workers, between June and September 1998.

In Glasgow interviews were carried out by the street outreach team of the Glasgow City Centre Initiative: in London by outreach workers from St Mungo's Association and the London Connection: and, in Swansea by the street outreach team of Caer Las Cyf.

- Front-Line Voluntary Sector Agencies
  - two sessions involving the major front-line voluntary sector agencies were conducted at each location (a list of participating organisations is set out in Appendix II)
  - a scoping session explored the key local issues on victimisation, offending and policing street homelessness

A sector development session examined local good practice and set out what needed to be done to tackle victimisation, reduce offending and potentially improve the policing of rough-sleepers

- Police
    - 53 UK Police Forces were surveyed by postal survey on policing policy, policing practice, local strategy on street homelessness, training, multi-agency work and desired changes in policing street homelessness (45 forces took part)
    - group discussions were undertaken involving 24 officers of varying rank
    - 35 one-to-one discussions were undertaken with police senior management, city centre operational management and front-line police officers

A national feedback and discussion seminar attended by 38 representatives was held in November 1998. Participants considered the initial findings and potential priorities for tackling victimisation, reducing offending and developing policing policy and practices.

Appendix II: participating organisations

The following agencies and organisations took part in or supported the investigation:

Glasgow

Big Issue in Scotland
GCSH (Glasgow Council for Single Homeless)
Glasgow City Centre Initiative
Wellpark Centre
Scottish Council for Single Homeless
Shelter Scotland
Simon Community
Strathclyde Police

London

Alone in London
Big Issue Foundation
Centrepoint Soho
Crisis
Homeless Network
Metropolitan Police
NCH – Action for Children
Providence Row
Revolving Doors Agency
Shelter
St Mungo's Association
Thamesreach Housing Association
The London Connection

Swansea

Barnardo's
Big Issue Cymru
Caer Las Cyf
Shelter Cymru
The Cyrenians
University of Swansea
(45 Police Forces responded to the Policing Policy Review)